Ashley Carus-Wilson

Tokiwa

And Other Poems

Ashley Carus-Wilson

Tokiwa
And Other Poems

ISBN/EAN: 9783744711470

Printed in Europe, USA, Canada, Australia, Japan

Cover: Foto ©Thomas Meinert / pixelio.de

More available books at **www.hansebooks.com**

TOKIWA

AND OTHER POEMS

BY MRS.

ASHLEY CARUS-WILSON

(MARY L. G. PETRIE, B.A. Lond.)

London

HODDER AND STOUGHTON

27, PATERNOSTER ROW

MDCCCXCV

TO IRENE

THE poet-painter's heaven-taught eye could see
  An angel, then a human face he sought
Through which God's radiant messenger might be
  Shown to his fellows ; and the image caught
  In a child they called " the Sunbeam." So he wrought
Two poem-pictures of the little maid,
  One as the blue-eyed playmate he had taught,
One as his visioned angel ; and displayed
On both one word, her name, *Peace,* as in Greek 'tis said.

The prophet-painter's heaven-taught eye had seen
  That child's high destiny, when her he drew
With bright hair flowing over robes of sheen
  Gilding the distant landscape's sombre hue ;
  And seven stars—light's perfection—in the blue
Of heaven above her brow ; and in her hands
  The cross-clasped Book of highest truth she knew,
And virgin Lily that unconquered stands
Till purity and truth have cleansèd all the lands.

True artist, like true poet, is a seer ;
  He sees, and makes us see, the tender rays
That lit a vanished past, and he can hear,
  As prophet, music of the coming days ;
  Reading a life-work in a child's rapt gaze.
My eyes upon his painting, my heart goes
  With that fair child, grown woman, as she lays
At God's feet all she is and has, for those
Hailing her their Peace-Angel 'mid the Himalayan snows.

v

CONTENTS

I

TALES OF THE EAST

TOKIWA

A STORY OF OLD JAPAN

ARGUMENT.—In A.D. 1159 there was war in Japan between two great feudal clans, the Hei or Taira, whose banners were red, and the Gen or Minamoto, whose banners were white. Yoshitomo, the Gen chief, was defeated and slain; and his three little sons escaped with their mother Tokiwa, the fairest woman in Japan. Availing himself of the Japanese belief that any deed done for a parent's sake is justifiable, Kiyomori, the victorious Hei chief, got his rival's sons into his power, and then, by equally cruel stratagem, used her maternal love to get possession of Tokiwa herself. Her youngest son, Ushiwaka or Yoshitsune, afterwards became the great national hero and first shogun of Japan.

The poem opens with allusion to the national custom of the Nagami or Beholding, when all go forth to view the successive spring blossoms and to make holiday. The plum, "snow in spring," is the emblem of enduring love, and is worn at marriages to remind the bridal pair that the trials and difficulties of their future life must be overcome by love. "O Ume" (Lady Plum Blossom) is a favourite appellation.

TOKIWA

A STORY OF OLD JAPAN

Snow in spring, a scented snow of blossom, white
  as Fuji-San

When his peak gleams in the sunshine, godlike
  guardian of Japan ;

Rosy then as dawn's first glow, when to the
  audacious plum succeeds

Lavish cherry, till chrysanthemum the bright
  procession leads,

Many-hued ; and last the maple blushes, like the
  parting day

Ere the summer fades, and all the world has gone
  upon its way

To each season's gay Nagami, to behold and to
  rejoice.

4

As I once rejoiced, when I had learned to know
  my Hero's voice,
When the mighty Yoshitomo crowned my hair
  with earliest plum,
Bursting forth, prophetic herald of the balmy days
  to come,
Ere a blade of grass was stirring, emblem meet
  of deathless love.
Thus he spake, " O Ume, Lady Blossom, thee I
  throne above
All the maidens of Dai-Nippon, fairest fair I place
  beside
Bravest brave, by Minamoto clan's great chieftain,
  chosen, tried ! "

Snow in spring, a chilling snow, that buried all
  the tender bloom
Of my girlhood, when my year was young, within
  a living tomb,

On that night when all was lost, and through the
death-strewn battle-field,

Where his elder sons had fallen, I sought madly,
till I kneeled

'Mid the torn and trampled banners of the
Minamoto host,

'Neath the spring-clad plum that from its blanched
and wavering branches tossed

Weightless burden of fair bloom on him, whose
dauntless heart was riven

By the traitor's stab; and overhead the dazzling
eyes of heaven

Gazed in myriads, distant, clear and calm, sole
witness of my grief.

Had the skies wept one tear with me, I had wept
and found relief.

Now my hot heart throbbed upon his breast, and
all my passion's glow

Left that cold and still ; Love's light was quenched,
and drifts of icy snow

Lay upon my life for aye ; the glorious sun, that
  wakes to reign

O'er Dai-Nippon first of all lands, cannot thaw my
  heart again.

So I closed my Hero's sightless eyes, that met
  the stars' cold gaze,

And I fled through frosty bye-paths from the
  fury of the Heis

With the babes to whom our love gave life. My
  first-born bore the weight

Of his father's sword, thus rescued from the foe's
  exultant hate ;

To my robe the second clung ; the youngest lay
  upon my breast,

Ushiwaka, at whose birth the prophets hailed me
  mother blest :

He should be our greatest warrior, greater even
  than his sire.

Thus we fled, and found a refuge from the
  pitiless desire

Of the dastard Kiyomori to destroy our name and
  race ;
And he knows not, till I tell him, where his rival's
  sons find grace.

Snow in spring.   They say that 'neath the gleaming cone of Fuji-San
Quenchless fires have raged, and smoking streams
  of molten lava ran
Down his trembling sides in days of yore.   So,
  though the snow lies cold
On my widowed heart, fierce flames of conflict
  burn there uncontrolled
Since the cruel Kiyomori sent this message through
  the land,
" Wheresoever she be hidden, let Tokiwa understand
That her mother lies in durance at Kiyoto, yet is
  freed
When the sons of Yoshitomo for her life and safety
  plead."

So he bribes me to betray my own sweet babes ;
for I must give

All I have, yea, even my sons, that she who gave
me life may live.

He will slay them, he has vowed it, to secure his
hard-won sway ;

Though I dreamed that Ushiwaka should avenge
our fall one day ;

As Yoshitsune the gallant should live on from age
to age,

Owned Dai-Nippon's foremost hero, wisest soldier,
warlike sage.

Dream as false as was my childhood's dream that
I should live to wed—

I, a peasant maid—two mighty chiefs : white Gen
and Taira red,

Hating each the other, both should love in me the
fairest fair.

Nay, they love not twice, who love as I loved him
beyond compare ;

And his widow still is happier than the great
    Mikado's wife.

Happier, were it not that I can only save his
    children's life

If my mother's blood is on my head, to stain my
    wretched soul

With that blackest stain that cuts it off for ever
    from its goal.

O my mother, live! and tell the gods (if gods can
    reign, and see

Such dire anguish and refuse to aid) how I have
    honoured thee.

I in mountain-girt Kiyoto go to death, and just implore,

"Slay me, ere I see my children's blood bedew the
    tyrant's floor."

Snow in spring, sweet snow of love's first bloom,
    cold snow of love bereft,

Snow that shrouded fires of strife, that veils white
    ashes that are left

After all these fires die down, and I live on for
keener pain,

I live on to curse my beauty, and to long for death
in vain.

Kiyomori's wrath was fearsome, yet I sought his
palace gate.

There he offered me his love, more hateful than
his direst hate :

He who basely slew the man he feared, and won
that fatal fight,

He who planned my children's slaughter thro' my
mother's sacred right,

Offers life to my fair sons, if I will give myself for
price.

Not myself; nay, what I gave before is never given
twice :

For my bosom hath no second shrine, can own no
second lord.

So I spurned him, and he seized the babes. My
mother then implored,

"Yield, and spare us! Kiyomori loves his fairest
captive well.

Loyal daughter, loyal mother, let the after ages
tell

How the chief of Hei had wide domain, yet owned
thy gentle rule."

Rather, how he made my anguish of his base
designs the tool.

Once I gave myself away, and had a higher self
for prize :

Now I sell me, body and soul, and am contemned
in my own eyes.

I could sell them for my mother ; I can sell myself
for them.

Come and weep the barter with me, ere ye rise up
to condemn

Me, as faithless to my first love. Make my burial
wet with tears ;

For I die to-day, although my wraith live on for
many years,

Haunting still its old abodes, apart from him I
　　loved alone.

Pity me, ye men, if ever ye a maid's true love
　　have known.

Pity me, ye women, ye who know how woman's
　　heart can ache,

Ye who loved and lost, and ye who loved and have,
　　whose love doth make

All your life a bower of singing birds, as sweet as
　　Fuji-San

When the thrushes crowd its thickets.   Pity, if
　　indeed ye can.

Pity me, ye gods.   To merciful Kwannon I used
　　to kneel,

Asking lover, asking son, at wayside shrines.   But
　　can she feel ?

Ye know nought of human sorrow, O ye radiant
　　ones above,

Ye were never born of woman, ye have tholed no
　　ruined love.

Stay, they told me in my childhood a dim
legend of the West,

How, a thousand years ago, there lay upon a
maiden's breast

He who made the world and would redeem mankind. A strange, old tale!

Were there such a God, I could endure; now I
can only wail.

Fuji-San, otherwise called Fuji-Yama, the lofty mountain which
dominates Japanese landscape, is described in a Japanese poem as
"a god-like protector watching over Japan." Dai Nippon, i.e.
"Great Japan," is the correct name of the whole Empire
Kwannon is the popular Goddess of Mercy.

Meylan, a Dutch writer, says that in the middle of the first
Christian century an Indian sect arrived in the Land of the
Rising Sun and preached "the world's redemption through the
Son of a virgin."

MEÉGWAHUN

A BALLAD OF OLD KASHMIR

The story of Meégwahun—that is, "Dweller under the canopy of clouds"—is told in the *Rajataringini*, a very ancient Sanskrit account of the early Kashmirian dynasties. It also describes the draining of the Sahtisar Lake by Kashaf, with the aid of Vishnu, which produced the famous Valley of Kashmir, "Kashmir-junat-puzir"—that is, "equal to Paradise"—as the Orientals fondly name it. Himalaya means "Abode of Snow."

"FAIR is my daughter, and her dower
Is fairer than her face,
So his must be no common gifts
Who wins this damsel's grace."

Thus spake the King of Khuttar
On the confines of Tibet,
In the brave days of old Kashmir,
Which bards can ne'er forget.

Then all the region watered by
　The mighty streams that flow
From the untrodden realm of gods,
　The vast Abode of Snow,

Rang with the summons to attend
　A tourney held to prove
Who, bravest of the brave, could win
　That fairest lady's love.

Princes and chieftains great of name,
　In goodliest array,
Flocked to the city, keen to show
　Their prowess in the fray.

And some were envied, some were feared,
　And one was met with scorn,
For him no gaudy tent was pitched,
　No banners proudly borne.

" Whence cam'st thou in such humble guise ?
    Of whom art thou the son ? "
And he, unruffled, made reply,
    " Call me Meégwahun.

" Dweller beneath the canopy
    Of clouds, I plant my spear
Upon the open plain ; the vault
    Of heaven, calm and clear,

" Be my pavilion, till my arm
    Earn me a right to take
Name that once claimed a loyal love
    And made the cowards quake."

The hour arrived, the lists were set,
    The princess came to view
From out her lofty balcony
    The deeds the doughty do.

2

Of all the claimants for her hand,
The worthiest proved by far
One straight as is the poplar tree,
And stately as chenar ;

As swift as antelope and strong
As is the twelve-horned stag ;
And all the feats of other men
Behind his exploits lag.

Her choice is made, and when they say,
" This is the mate for her,"
Meégwahun declares himself
Son of Andjudeshtur.

The realm his fathers ruled was won
By Vishnu, as the prize
Of holy Kashaf's prayers, to be
The earthly Paradise.

Its ramparts are eternal hills
  Whose snows perpetual feed
The winding Jhelum, gladdening it
  With garden, tilth, and mead.

But many a day this fair Kashmir
  To aliens had been thrall,
So now they sought their monarch's heir
  And prayed him rule them all.

Meégwahun went forth from thence
  To conquer far and wide,
From Sindhu's source to warm Ceylon,
  And all his foes defied.

Valour and beauty made our land
  As proud as it was fair ;
Valour and beauty are decayed
  Beneath the yoke we bear.

The gloomy Moslem pens our dames
In jealous *purdah* now ;
And writes his *kismet*, baffling deed,
On every manly brow.

I sing this song of olden days
When we were strong and free,
To show what men there were of yore,
And shame the men that be.

II

SONGS OF LOVE AND HOME

THE LAD THAT I LUVE WEEL

THEY tell't me that my face is fair,
  They luved me dear as life :
But not a lad amang them a'
  Could win me to his wife.

The breeze that wanders o'er the brae
  A joy in blawin' finds
Strange to the faint an' prisoned air
  About the city wynds.

Sae fettered is the wedded life,
  Sae free is maidenhood ;
An' I luved liberty fu' weel,
  An' wadna doff the snood,

Till Charlie cam' adoun the glen,
An' I was proud to see
The brawest lad in a' the land
Had een for nane but me.

An' when I knew his gentle soul
He touched my heart beside ;
I gi'ed him luve for luve, an' said,
Oh, daur I be his bride ?

But trust cam' followin' hard on luve,
I found him leal as gold ;
Then freedom grew a fashous thing,
An' bonds were joy untold.

An' now I gie thee a' my heart,
O strang an' true an' good !
I meekly don the coif for thee
An' doff my maiden snood.

TO SEA !

" O'ER the bounding main the breezes sweep,

The sea birds are calling across the deep,

The laughing billows dance and play,

The good ship ploughs her unswerving way.

O Love, who art all the world to me,

Come with me, come with me, over the sea."

" Can I leave the soft warm nest where I dwell,

The kith and the kin who love me well ?

Can I cross a strange sea to a stranger strand,

And live a new life in a foreign land ?

Yea, over the ocean with thee I come,

For wherever my Love is, there is Home."

LIFE'S WINTER

I STOOD by the shore of the summer sea :
   The tide sang songs to the breeze,
And my heart was as glad as the leaves that clad
   The waving summer trees ;
For a new tide of love rushed over me,
Bright as the tide of the summer sea.

I stood by the shore of the winter sea :
   The blast was wet with spray ;
And dark and cold the waters rolled,
   And my heart cried, " Well away ! "
For a lonely anguish swept over me,
Wild as the waves of the winter sea.

I stood again by the summer sea :

    It smiled, unchanged by the storm ;

But my heart so true was shadowed anew

    By its grief in a darker form.

O Earth ever fair ! O ageless Sea !

Can there be only one summer for me ?

LIFE'S SUMMER

SUNSHINE of earliest spring had kissed the earth
And made it smile anew with tender green,
When birdlings twittering as they built their nests
Told me Love is, though Love I had not seen.

Hawthorns decked mead and copse with flame and
    snow,
Fresh foliage waved rejoicing in the grove,
When songsters soaring, shrilling carols gay,
Told me the sweetest thing on earth is Love.

When glowing summer after balmy spring
Strewed every hedge with blushing eglantine,
One came to me as bright as summer sun,
And murmured in my ear that Love is mine.

Dawn followed hard on twilight when I gave
Promise that made midsummer in my soul ;
And o'er it strange, warm waves of new delight,
Far sweeter than the Love I dreamed of, roll.

Hushed were the birds when seeking Love's first
    song
Gave place to the sweet silence of Love won ;
And on our plighted troth God's blessing came
With sultry air and waning summer sun.

Now he is mine and I am wholly his.
The woods are gold and crimson ere they fall ;
Quick-coming winter saddens earth, but me
The joys of changeless summer still enthrall ;

For ever o'er our blended lives there broods,
With golden pinions and with fragrant breath,
Filling our hearts with music and with mirth,
Pure, passionate, patient Love that outlives death.

BETROTHED

He. " GIVE me the ring I gave, love,
        Hoping to give thee bliss.
    And one last boon I crave, love,
        From thy pure lips a kiss ;
That I may remember through griefs to come
The vanishing light of my heart's dear home.

        " As thou wouldst kiss the dead, love,
        Sealing the breathless lips,
    For slumber without a dread, love,
        Hallowing life's eclipse.
Go, live the life that thou livedst before,
And think not of me on the exile's shore."

30

She. " I give thee the ring ; but endeavour

　　　Recalleth its vow in vain ;

　　　Love that is thine for ever

　　　Cannot return again.

I was mine and God's : I am God's and thine.

The love in thine eyes is my soul's sunshine.

　　" Ne'er again will the seasons

　　　Restore the virgin heart,

　　　Dimly pondering its treasons,

　　　Single, sitting apart :

And doubting that Love were more than a name,

Until Love, light-bearing and radiant, came ;

　　" My empty life fulfilling,

　　　Making its purpose great ;

　　　How can my soul be willing

　　　To make it desolate ?

For earth's dearest treasure in Love I own,

And I dread no life but the life alone.

"Exile is no denial
    If I am by thy side ;
Penury hath no trial
    If thou with me abide.
Far poorer than thou art thou leavest me,
Thou takest my heart and my life with thee."

WEDDED

WHAT can I give, O dearest one, to thee,

To whom my life doth set itself, like words

That were not known as sweet till answering

chords

Of music swept them into song ?   For free

Thou, as a king, bestowedst regally

The greatest thing a human creature hoards,

The unmeasured gift wealth only once affords,

The priceless gift of thy heart's love on me.

And I to thee, thy love creating mine,

Poured forth pure gold unweighed in recompense.

Now have I nought to give, till my receipt

Of new love from thy love, grown more intense,

Bring me fresh gifts to lavish at thy feet.

So all of mine that is not God's, is thine.

LOVING LIPS

DEAR lips, that won my love with thy soft speech,
   Wakening youth and hope to sudden song,
   And claimed me thine for ever with the long
Sweet kiss of our betrothal ; we beseech
Remembrance of our last embrace may reach
   From farewell unto greeting, that no wrong
   Be done to love by parting, but among
Life's tumult we be sealèd, each for each.

   Dearer lips now that thou and I are one,
And tread life's path together, smooth and steep,
   (Like rivers travelling in one calm stream
   That mingled foaming, roaring, gleam on gleam).
For uttering only kindness, thou dost keep
   All thou didst win till life and love are done.

LIFE AND LOVE

In the spring of my life and the year,
Through a newly robed glade there drew near
A sweet maiden, surpassingly fair,
    In her arms bearing daffodils meek,
With the light of the sun in her hair,
    And the hue of the spring on her cheek.
Then I loved, wooed and won her, and cried,
" Love never flowed in so full a tide ! "

In the winter of life and the year,
We together await without fear
Lasting life beyond this little life.
    Firelight flickers on hair like new snow,
Wan and weak are the hands of my wife.
    Can Time mock at the love long ago ?
Rather, Love hath the might of the sea,
Broadening on in the broader To Be.

TWO LOVES

HE loves me as he never loved before.

He loved me till he had my love again,

And each taught other Love's enchanting lore,

Set to an ever new and glad refrain.

Light whence the clouds of yesterday depart,

To-day's fair noon, the Husband of my heart.

I love him as I never loved before.

I love him, waiting for his love again,

Till, loving me, he Love's first path explore,

Waking on life set to its sweetest strain ;

Seal of my first love, pledge of two made one,

To-morrow's daystar, infant firstborn Son.

36

MOTHER AND CHILD

I. OCTOBER 11TH, 186-.

MOTHER and Child.

The mother trembles : her hour hath come,

On the mystic confines of death and life ;

Then joys in a gift of all gifts the sum,

In a babe who weeps, new born to the strife ;

But bringing a blessing large and whole,

Flesh of thy flesh and soul of thy soul.

O sweetest outcome of human love !

The pang is o'er, waft thy praise above,

Happy Mother and wailing Child.

37

II.   APRIL 4TH, 187–.

Mother and Child.

The child is trembling : her hour hath come,
  On the mystic confines of life and death ;
For leaving the love of her earthly home,
  Alone in the darkness she yields her breath
Bound for the light of eternal peace ;
While the stricken mother's tears increase.
O woeful outcome of human sin !
The pang is o'er, let thy grief begin.

Wailing Mother and happy Child.

III. January 31st, 188–.

Mother and Child.

The mother gives thanks : her hour hath come,

On the mystic confines of death and life ;

From the dying children, whose pain is dumb,

Left alone to strive and to finish their strife,

She goes to the living child, who waits

For her till their Lord unlock the gates.

O blessed outcome of love Divine !

The pang is o'er and Paradise thine.

Happy Mother and happy Child.

BABY'S LAST SLEEP

A TRUE INCIDENT, RELATED IN WORDSWORTH'S

"POSTSCRIPT" 1835

WELL, ye have hunted to earth your prey,

Guardians of law that we must obey ;

Prey that turns not again to rend,

A weary woman without a friend,

Who was once a mother,

And sought to smother

Her fugitive sob until life had end.

"Where did I hide it ?   Why did I keep it ? "

" Feared I not law that I dared to o'erleap it ? "

40

" The Parish provideth the means and the room,

Granteth its paupers their nameless tomb."

> Only once a mother,

> I had ne'er another !

Could I give my darling to such a doom ?

As an armèd man our poverty came,

Rifled our joys and branded our name.

Labour for living, for raiment and meat,

Drained life of all that maketh it sweet.

> Yet our baby's voice

> Bade our hearts rejoice ;

For her would we toil through burden and heat.

Only for work then my husband implored.

O God ! that in England, with riches stored,

The able hand and the willing heart

Vainly offer their toil in the mart,

> While the withering wife

> Leads an anguished life,

As bread-winner missing the mother's part !

Weary tramp for uncertain wage,

Wakeful hours that swept youth into age,

Lack of fuel in frost and in rain,

Lack of care in my peril and pain

Wasted my force

From its inmost source,

And I took my babe to my bosom in vain.

She died, whom I toiled for till eyes were dim,

Till knees were trembling and brain did swim ;

The only ray in my sky storm-riven,

For whom my life had been well-nigh given.

How could I endure

The grave of the poor

For that fair little shrine of a soul in Heaven ?

So I hid my baby away and cried,

" Day and night will I toil to provide

Enough to lay my child in the sod

Under the shade of the holy rood,

That when earth doth quake

And the sleepers awake

Her name may appeal to the children's God!"

We carried that coffer as dire want chased

From attic to cellar in trouble and haste.

We feared not that presence of Death where we dwelt,

But her helpless warmth at my heart I felt

Once again in dreams

When the moon's pale beams

Silvered the ark where I daily knelt.

Then came sickness and substance pawned,

And relentless gates of the workhouse yawned.

Till I was a widow with rent unpaid,

And my all was seized and discovery made.

Poor-house hinges swung,

And my death-knell rung,

Above ground, lifeless yet restless, laid.

Away from her spirit that cannot perish!

Away from the dust that I fain would cherish!

You tell me I rave with an erring tongue.

Ah! Ye know not the wandering fancies that
throng

When the pulses fail

And the lips are pale,

And lonely hunger and anguish long.

Give me a grave where my babe may rest

Once again on her mother's breast.

For she never knew a harsher bed,

Though we were hungry and hard bestead.

She will wake and cry

When I am not nigh

If you nail that rough plank o'er her little head.

MY ONLY ONE

SUGGESTED BY BARONESS STACKELBERG'S LIFE OF "CARMEN SYLVA," QUEEN OF ROUMANIA

FROM the home whose sweetest music was her
    voice,
  From the arms where her golden head nestled
They have borne her; so let joyless Death
    rejoice,
  Since in vain with him she wrestled.
    When cometh the spring,
    Young birds will sing
O'er the grave where my child is hushed.
    From the rock below,
    Where the sun kissed the snow,
A gay little brook will have gushed,

With its gossip light,

As it dances bright

Morns, noons, and eves,

To the opening leaves,

Of its journey adown the hill,

O'er the grave where my child is still.

Never she stirs in her sleep,

Never she smiles in her dreams

With her face one deep

Sweet flush, wakes to leap

To my arms, when the beams

Of the morning peep.

Flower, field, forest will borrow

A new life from the sun,

While I lie down in sorrow

Till all my course is run,

With ever a desolate morrow,

She was my Only One.

Ye pass me by

With undimmed eye

Childless ones, who have never borne a child.

The unremembered anguish drowned in joy,

The living for another life's employ

Never thrilled you with its rapture, ne'er beguiled

From the selfish quest,

From the aimless rest ;

Never stirred the even tenor of your course.

Have ye lain down in the dust with wailing
mad,

Seen the sun that ruled your days in sackcloth
clad,

When from your warm breast, Death, knowing no
remorse,

Hid your babe in earth's cold cradle? Nay, ye
miss

All the deepest woe that falls on woman's heart ;

All that hungry longing dying in despair

For one fondling touch, one glint of golden hair,

One appealing cry, one generous, eager kiss ;

All that deepest joy that leaveth keenest smart,

Baffled promise, shrouded hopes,

Darkness where my spirit gropes.

Do I envy you your calm and painless days?

This I asked my heart one morn in sore amaze

When to church I went,

With night's weeping spent,

To kneel to the unseen Christ,

Who for us was sacrificed ;

To receive His Holy Bread,

To think of the blessed dead.

Then I cried up to Christ to comfort me

Till my mourning changed to Eucharist.

For God loved better, though I love well,

So He took my child with Him to dwell.

When her lips had learned to frame

For me, one matchless name.

She is mine for all eternity.

Yea, I am a Mother for evermore.

Small price for such joy was the pain I bore.

As the blessed Galilean Maid

Was a mother still when her Son was laid

In Joseph's tomb, since He rose and restored

Life and love beyond this life,

Dimmed with sorrow, marred with strife,

And I still can praise and thank Thee, Lord,

Till my shadowed course is run,

That I had my Only One.

"AND THE BABE WEPT"

BORN into this strange world to-night, poor Babe,
Thine earliest language is a cry of pain,
Uttering thine unknown helplessness and need,
A cry that wakens Love and brings thee aid.

Thy mother's arms have gathered thee, sweet Babe,
And thou art smiling, for, unknown to thee,
Earth's greatest treasure is thine own in love.
O happy love and happier trust, that build
The fairy palace of our childhood's bliss!

Thrust into life from sheltering wings of home,
Or finding love transferred to newer claims,
Thy cry of lonely pain goes forth once more,
Wakening a stronger Love than mother's love.

God gathers thee in His almighty arms,

And thou dost smile, for, not unknown to thee,

Heaven's crown of joy is thine in Love Divine.

O conquering faith and unconfounded hope,

The sure foundations of abiding bliss!

III

TALES OF GREECE

ORPHEUS BEREFT

"Ipse, cava solans ægrum testudine amorem,
  Te, dulcis conjux, te, solo in littore secum,
  Te, veniente die, te, decedente, canebat."

VERGIL, *Georg. IV.*, 464

EURYDICE ! Eurydice !

" King of singers ! " they cry to me.

Where is the man that of fame hath more ?

Where is the man that is left with less

Of all that could give it power to bless ?

Here I wander beside the shore,

Desolate shore of a moaning sea.

Eurydice ! Eurydice !

55

Plaudits are sweet when they reach an ear

That garners them up for one held dear ;

Plaudits are but an added pain

To him who never will hear again

The voice that summed up sweet music's whole

Into one grand chord to entrance my soul.

Away from plaudits unshared by thee,

I mourn by the marge of the mourning sea.

    Eurydice ! Eurydice !

Phœbus gave me my magic lyre,

Thoughts, words, and voice that were touched with

    fire.

Then I dreamed my dream of a poet's sway

Over human hearts ; when my kindling lay

Roused passion and tears and heroic deed,

Power and fame were my ample meed ;

Till a strange new longing was stirred in me,

I could barter them both for a smile from thee,

    Eurydice ! Eurydice !

Then I loved not my lyre because Phœbus gave,

And the Muses taught me beside the wave

Of bright Hippocrene to wake its strings;

But because it could bear me away on the
  wings

Of a soaring hope that made all things new,

And could call to thy cheek a responsive hue

When it uttered ineffable love for thee,

My love, and my wife that was to be,

  Eurydice! Eurydice!

.

A serpent wounded thy searching hand

As thou gatheredst flowers on sunlit land.

Then Hades claimed thee, earth's brightest bloom,

For the realm of shades and the hungry tomb.

But Love led me down, while I yet had breath,

To charm with my lyre even bloodless Death.

Till Pluto gave heed to my passionate plea,

" Thou hast maidens enow, set my maiden free!"

  Eurydice! Eurydice!

So upward we journeyed, the damsel wan
Who had passed through death, and the living
  man
Who had plunged from sunshine to nether night,
To face its shadows and dare its might
In the greater might of a deathless love,
For her who had left him in darkness above.
Out of Hades she followed me,
Faint footstep, fair form that I must not see,
    Eurydice ! Eurydice !

When we reached the threshold I heard no more
Her light foot falling on Pluto's floor.
The wind of heaven was kissing my face—
Did she follow still ?—Thus the hard-won grace
Was lost by a fear, by a doubt, by a glance ;
My pact was broken, and forfeit our chance.
Snatched from life and sunshine and liberty,
I saw her stretch her white arms to me,
    Eurydice ! Eurydice !

" King of singers ! " they cry to me.

Sorrow of heart makes my song more sweet,

Like the nightingale's lay that will soon be shed

O'er the grave of a poet whom gods endowed

With a bliss that has melted like morning cloud,

And a fame that survives, with its garlands dead

And its shouts that louder and louder greet

Him who only lived in his love for thee,

  Eurydice ! Eurydice !

LOXIAS

ξυναινέσασα Λοξίαν ἐψευσάμην.—ÆSCHYLUS, *Agamemnon*, 1208

THE lives of men are woven with the thread
Of love and sorrow, and we gods who dwell
On high Olympus know them too, 'tis said.

For love, the light of heaven, doth cast her spell
Upon us, and the shadow of that light
Is grief for human creatures we love well.

She that I loved with all a god's great might
Refused the love I meant to be her crown,
And turned it to a halter for her white

Round throat, and mine is sorrow not my own.
Cassandra, fairest virgin of thy race,
I have destroyed thee, I have cast thee down.

A child, thou slumberest in my holy place.

I came to thee, I taught thee things divine ;

While each new year adorned thee with new
grace.

Then when the charms of womanhood were
thine

I clad me as a simple shepherd swain,

I found thee at a lonely woodland shrine,

I poured out love I could no more refrain ;

And thou didst promise to be mine alone.

But when with godlike gifts I came again

To claim thy plighted troth, Apollo shone

Upon thy gaze. Thou stood'st in dumb surprise,

Thy warm arms folded o'er thy jewelled zone,

One moment, then from out thy radiant eyes

The princess flashed, " Thy gifts be to another."

And then the shrinking woman kneels and cries,

" Blast me not with thy splendours, for no other

Than mortal fires can kindle this poor breast.

I am no Semele, that I should smother

My fears in my ambition, ask as guest

Thunder-clad gods. I pray thee, let me go."

So dear art thou, that dear was thy behest ;

And thou dost fly, as flies a milk-white doe

Through brake and forest from the foaming
hound.

For peerless beauty and for peerless woe

In song and story must thou be renowned.

For unto thee the fatal gift was given

When my eye, kindling with its passion, found

Response in thine, and thought its suit had thriven.

Grief must be thine no healing can remove,

Till with the sword thy tender heart is riven.

Oh, would that thou hadst given me thy love!

Then I had taught thee songs that should have
    won

The world to listen to the tale we wove.

Now thou shalt prophesy in Troy, and none

Shall hearken to the words the gods inspire;

And, ere the undoing, thou shalt see undone

Thy father's house, and feel the raging fire

That wraps the city in its crimson shroud,

Helpless to avert, though sickening with desire.

To thee, beneath the double anguish bowed,

Sweet love, that lighteneth all the load of life,

Can never give relief; for of the crowd

Of fellow-mortals, who could call thee wife,

Thee, who hadst known a god? Nay, highest
    things,

Seen but not grasped, leave heaven and earth at
    strife,

Earth's glory pale, and heaven beyond thy wings,

And keener pains, with keener sense of pain.

Now, in the triumph of the avenging Kings,

I see thee, 'mid the slayers and the slain,

Fly to the temple from the mad turmoil,

Seeking Athene's sanctuary in vain ;

I see thee led, as Ilion's fairest spoil,

To Greece, to chant thy wild prophetic song,

Swan-like, ere death ; I see thy frame recoil

From horrid visions, that upon thee throng,

Of violence, teeming with its sinful brood ;

Praying the agony may not be long,

Which rends the life from thy fair flesh, endued

With god-loved grace ; I see thy throbbing brow

Dashed on the floor that soon shall drink thy
blood

ISMENE

A TALE OF SPARTA, B.C. 479

" ISMENE," women shouted, as the damsel hastened
  by;

" Ismene, art thou raving?"   But wingless was the
  cry.

" She sobbed and beat her bosom when alive he
  came again,

Not a tear had she to give him when we told her
  he was slain ;

But with wild eyes, like a Mænad mantled in a
  leopard's hide,

Drank she, as a draught of nectar, our news of how
  he died."

Her snowy peplus fluttering, her rippling locks
  unbound,

She flees from all the voices, she seeks the sacred
  ground,

The grotto of Apollo, where the god in marble
  stands

By a shadow-fretted stream, enriching wide Laco-
  nian lands.

With arms stretched down and fingers twined and
  palms towards the sod,

And upward gaze, Ismene tells her story to the
  god.

" O radiant Son of Leto, lover of the Dorian
  race,

Let me snap the chains of silence in this well-
  beloved place.

'Tell me what is Eros like, Leukippe?' asked I
  once, and she

Fondling said, ' Be good, my flowcret, and some
  day thou shalt see !'

From the one child in the household such questions
  often burst,
Fruit of lone and shadowy ponderings and wonder
  longtime nursed,
Till the vagueness and the vastness of the thoughts
  I would explore
Loosed my lips, to gain an answer that scaled them
  evermore.
I was scolded for a fault and murmured, full of
  shame, ' Oh, would
That I, like those around me, were full-grown and
  always good !
Now, to my childish vision the world was passing
  fair,
And all men wise and good ; but wise and good
  beyond compare
Were Lycophron, the lawyer, and the seer,
  Megistias.
Till when the springtide sun had drawn first
  shadows o'er the grass

I found my flowers, childhood's friends, in all their
   infant bloom,
Slain by a curse that Winter hurled from out her
   ice-bound tomb.
A yet more blasting wind I felt, stirred by an idle
   tongue,
'Lycophron's clever, but a knave; 'tis so with half
   the young ;
And worthy old Megistias dotes.'   Thus grieved at
   heart I grew ;'
Can Nature mar her fairest handiwork, and is it
   true
That others stumble like myself, and dreams are
   only dreams?
They roused me from my musings, which would
   blur my brow with seams
Unfit for such a fair young head, for girls were
   made to please ;
To love and be beloved, to all their problems were
   the keys.

Then sunshine flooded all my life : I was beloved
    by one,

In whom my lost ideal of the human creature
    shone.

Much had he, lovelit eyes gave all to him ; and
    then I poured

Forth the rich treasure of my maiden love, and
    called him lord.

Proud were my tears when first he went to glory
    in the field :

'On it, or with it,' cried his mother, as he raised
    the shield.

So came the famous fight, concerning which the
    minstrels sing,

When the Three Hundred flouted all the myriads
    of the King.

At the Gates of Greece they gathered ; there they
    fought and there they fell,

Megistias, Maron, Alphæus, and Dienekes, as
    well

As the Thespian Dithyrambus, have their names
  engraved in brass :
They flinched not when the traitor came upon them
  from the Pass ;
But flung the spear, drew sword, and thrust the
  dagger to and fro,
Then, like bloodhounds at a hunting, tore with
  tooth and nail the foe.
Through the wooded glens of Oeta rang the groans
  that rescued Greece,
And the vanquished were victorious in her dearly
  won release.
Where was Aristodemus on that memorable
  day ?
Faint 'neath a load of sickness, he at fair Alpeni
  lay ;
But thence his comrade Eurytus struggled to death
  and fame ;
While he returned to Sparta safe and overwhelmed
  with shame.

'Weep not; he was not worthy. Dear girl, the
world is wide :

We'll find a nobler Spartan, and thou shalt be his
bride.'

Thus they comforted my sorrow; it was all they
understood ;

And stunned, I sought the shadows of the bright-
haired Archer's wood.

Truly the gods have mocked us; for our vehement
desire

Makes us dream that others reach the goal, that
we alone aspire.

Time, robbing of the many, leaves us still the one
whom we

Dower with all graces as the god of our
idolatry.

'Tis thus men worship women, and thus women
worship men ;

And Eros is like this; while we, who live beneath
the ken

Of all Olympus, rouse the laughter of the immortal
    Powers,

' Why, men would be as gods, were all things theirs
    as well as ours.

And still we yearn and still we clothe our God in
    human form.

Athens has Pallas; Sparta, Phœbus : and the
    gaping swarm

By these may measure all their dull deformity and
    need.

But does our yearning shape these gods, or are
    there gods indeed ?

Homer says all men hunger for the gods.   Then
    we are blind,

And see them not, but seek on earth what we can
    never find.

So the fair idol I had wrought lay shattered for a year,

Till Hera heard our prayers and granted to the
    Dorian spear,

Between Platæa's bastions and Asopus' winding
river,

To hurl the foes of Hellas back for ever and for
ever.

And from that battle-field to me one long, dark
lock they bring,

Clotted with gore, and tell me how they wondering
saw him fling

Him singlehanded on the foe, until the deeds he
wrought

Said, 'Ares nerves his arm to fight as mortal never
fought.'

And by-and-by my tears will flow, when all my loss
I feel :

But now my maddened brain exults, my dazzled
senses reel.

I cannot fathom in my thinking, why we aim so
high,

And could I, what were worth to men the thoughts
of such as I ?

Perhaps thc Athenian sages understood it long ago ;

Or maybe these are secrets which we all must die
to know.

But my woman's heart is satisfied, although my
mind may crave ;

For in the gloom of Hades I shall find him with
the brave."

NOTE.—For the story of Aristodemus, who retrieved at Platæa
his failure at Thermopylæ, *see* Grote's "History of Greece," chaps.
XL., XLII. ; *see* also "Odyssey," III. 48.

THE TALE OF EPITHERSES THE GRAMMARIAN

As told in Plutarch's "De Oraculorum Defectu."

"WELL, I will tell you how Corcyra mourned
The great god Pan.   But ask me not to tell
Whether the gods can die, or why that voice
Came to Tamois.   I was pious once,
And pondered all these things, and freely gave
My substance for the sacrifice ; but now
Fairer than such dim piety I find
Obedience to the reverend law of Right
That gods like men must bow to ; and since they
Vex not their souls for us, I will not chafe
Mine to resolve the riddles they propound.

It was the nineteenth spring Tiberius reigned.

Men still rejoiced that Tiber's yellow wave

Rolled o'er Sejanus, praying a like hour

Might yet be his, who on the Caprean isle

Wore out his hideous dotage year by year.

Earth had awaked once more, and flocks and herds

Browsed with their yeanlings over hill and dale,

When I took ship and sailed for Italy ;

Laden with Greek books, which the Romans love

(You are a Hellene) as they love our wines,

Our slaves, our statues, pastimes for an hour,

Which only rich and idle can enjoy.

Prosperous breezes drove us through the Gulf

Of Corinth, past Naupactus with her forts,

To the Echinades, where Achelous,

King of Greek rivers, pours his sluggish stream

Into the main, and builds those islands up

Of Acarnanian and Ætolian soil.

And there the wind sank into sleep as deep

As the worn slave's whose master is abroad.

We furled the sails and trolled the rowers' lay,

And smote the yielding billow with our oars.

And so we came to Paxos, where we rode

At anchor, waiting for a southern gale.

The moon was full, and night and silence reigned,

But for the water lapping on the keel

With languid sway, more restful even than rest.

All slumbered, save the watch and Tamois,

The Egyptian pilot, when a sudden voice

Rang from the rocky island, clear and shrill :

'Tamois! Tamois!' But he answered not,

Startled and fearing either god or man.

Clearer and shriller rang the voice again :

'Tamois! Tamois!' So he made reply,

· What wouldest thou with me?' and heard the
   words,

'When thou arrivest at Phalacrum, shout,

Loud as thy lungs can speak, GREAT PAN IS
   DEAD.'

Then night and silence reigned on all around.

Panic and dim perplexity were ours ;

Impiety to scorn divine behest ;

Impiety to think a god could die.

'We need,' I said, ' another sign from heaven,'

(The morning wind was rising as I spake)

' If, when we see the headland, all our sails

Are swollen, we will pass, and let him find

Another herald ; but if it be calm—

Take courage, Tamois, breath is only breath.'

And then our skiff went bounding o'er the sea,

Measuring all Corcyra's western coast ;

Its vales gleamed green betwixt its rugged hills

Washed by the same blue ocean that once bore

Forlorn Odysseus to his bed of leaves

And kind Phæacian welcome.   As I thought

Of all our glorious past and Homer's tale,

The crisply curling waves had ceased to dance

And a calm sea mirrored a cloudless sky.

Phalacrum viewed its image in the deep,

As Tamois spake, his swart face blanched with
    fear,
His eyes set 'neath his low Egyptian brow,
' Current nor rock, nor shoal nor reef I dread
By your Greek isles, but I must fear your gods,
And cannot disobey them.'   With that word
He mounted on the prow and cried aloud,
' GREAT PAN IS DEAD.'   Forthwith arose a sound
From the Chaonian coast and countless isles,
As when the breath of angry Zeus hath stirred
The oaks of old Dodona, and his will
Is woe to men, or when the wind and sea
Uniting swell the dirge of all their dead.
So Nature wailed, and heralded a cry
Exceeding bitter, as from human lips,
Maddened by no mere sorrow, but despair,
No mere remorse, but never-dying shame.
Great Pan is dead, and we have done the deed.
Great Pan is dead, who lived through all the
    world

And made it fair and fertile with his life.

The vulgar tell their vulgar tales of Pan,

In twofold nature, for they could not know

The god we worship, even that same Power

Whom we call Pan, since It is everywhere

And kindles all creation with one Soul ;

Thought, Passion, Will in man ; in lower forms

Mere life that lives, moves and yields other life.

But though I saw and heard all this, I doubt,

If Pan be such, that Pan could ever die."

Thus Epitherses.   Then his hearer said,

" The wondrous tale you tell confounds me not.

There is a town in Syria where they slew,

The nineteenth spring Tiberius reigned in Rome,

One whose death agony upon the cross

Caused earth to quake and rocks to rend in twain,

And darkness over all the land at noon ;

Although the moon then rode full-orbed in heaven.

These signs and wonders were the works of GOD,

Wrought in the selfsame hour that yon Greek isles
Bewailing Pan, mourned for the death of Christ."

Said Epitherses, " I have heard of one
Christus or Chrestus, who stirred up the Jews,
And suffered death, which Rome awards to all
Who cannot bow their necks beneath her yoke.
Yea, some affirm that 'mid the city slaves
A senseless superstition lingers yet ;
They gather in the twilight dawn, and sing
Hymns to this Christ.   Maybe thou knowest more."

In hushed and solemn tones the answer came :
" Betray me not, and I will tell thee all.
I am His servant and I bear His Name ;
For I believe He is the Son of God,
Only-begotten, through whom all was made,
Who is the Life of all things, and who came,
Two-natured, Very God and Very Man,
Born of a Virgin, to redeem mankind

6

By His most righteous life and guiltless death ;

Whom Pilate crucified, but the third morn

He rose from death, ascending into Heaven ;

Whence He shall come again to judge the world

In righteousness, and every knee shall bow

And own Him Lord. Life's shadows lengthen out,

But still I pray that I may see one day

Dawn deepening into glory not its own,

His banner flaming in the eastern heaven,

And hear the shout that hails Him earth's true

King."

NOTE.—*Vide* TACITUS, *Annals* xv. 44; PLINY, *Epist.* x. 96 THUCYDIDES, ii. 84, 102.

IV

SONGS OF LIFE AND DEATH

THE LAST LEAF

"My days are in the yellow leaf."—*Byron*

SERE and solitary leaflet, fluttering on the naked
tree,

Last of all the clustering foliage that of old held
revelry,

Wintry winds are moaning dirges, as they sway
the weary bough,

Driving rains descend to dash thee on the lonely
highway now ;

Quickly fall and quickly perish, wrinkled relic of
the past !

Wherefore should we linger, grieving that the
summer cannot last ?

I have lived and loved and waited, till my fairest
hopes have fled ;
Lived till all I loved have left me envying the
untroubled dead.
I have lived till men contemn me, last of all my
name and race ;
Lived till they have jostled by me, pressing to a
higher place.
Generations follow ever, each his petty course to
run,
While the timeworn world rolls onward, round and
round the same old sun.
Memories of lost companions mock my eld like
spectres dim,
While their heedless sons carousing fill the goblet
to the brim.
Take me to thine aged bosom, Mother Earth from
whom I sprung,
For their revels cannot vex me when my funeral
knell hath rung.

Let the silent ferry bear me to the realm of shades,
for there
I may find my bitter spirit not alone in its
despair.

"EARTH TO EARTH"

"Mortalem vitam mors quum immortalis ademit"
LUCRETIUS, *De Rer. Nat.*, *III.* 882

THOU art wearied with the stir of strife, our
brother,
Dimmed are thine eyes and chill thy breast,
So we lay thee in the lap of Earth, thy Mother,
To slumber in never-ending rest.

Fear not, 'tis a sleep without a waking ;
Shrink not, no dreams can visit thee ;
No troubled dawn for thee is breaking ;
Lie down, from pain and struggle free.

88

Lie down ; thou canst not hear us weeping,

    Thou canst not see us as we mourn ;

And yet—Oh, would thou knewest we are keeping

    Love that can hope for no return !

Joy still is ours—to taste of sorrow ;

    Garlands we weave upon our brow—

Only to watch them fade to-morrow.

    Would we might sleep beside thee now !

No more from bliss to anguish swaying,

    Thy scale to centred calm hath swung.

And, were there gods, 'twere true, that saying,

    " Whom the gods love will perish young."

'ESSE EST PERCIPERE'

" Before us there is certainly only Nothingness. . . . Nothingness which we discern behind all virtue and holiness as their final
goal, and which we fear as children fear the dark. We must not
even evade it like the Indians, through myths and meaningless
words, such as re-absorption in Brahma, or the Nirvana of the
Buddhists."—SCHOPENHAUER, *Die Welt als Wille und Vorstellung*

VOICES and tumult and conflict ; hope and despair
   and pain,
Echoed and yet re-echoed. Oh, where were the
   mighty gain
Did they echo on for ever through worlds with
   being rife?
Sleep is sweeter than waking, and death is better
   than life.

When Vikings battled for plunder over the fields
of ice,

They dreamed in the pine-woods' gloom of a
heroes' paradise ;

Every day there was slaughter, and slain lived
again to slay,

Every night they feasted and drank the same
mead alway.

But I, of the world's old age, push from my sated
lips

A larger draught of life, and although the Future
eclipse

The Now in its power to please, it can offer nought
to me

That could satisfy my soul like the hope of Not
to Be.

I bury my face in sickness, longing with fevered
will

That the pulses of life may cease, that all be dark
and still.

Oh, sweet are the valley clods, when, worn with
the jar of earth,

Nirvana laps us in peace we were roused from at
our birth !

Nothing in Nature is lost, but all is combined
anew ;

Dissolve then this subtle web, from which our
consciousness grew.

Twilight gathers and deepens, and hushed is the
voice of strife ;

Sleep is sweeter than waking, and death is better
than life.

THE MUSIC OF LIFE

" Harmoniam Graii quam dicunt."—LUCRETIUS

A MAIDEN'S pure soul
Through the cadence stole
Where the linked notes meet
In a lyre most sweet ;
It wailed with woe and it thrilled with joy,
Under her fingers' benign employ.

Time the lyre will blast.
Can the music last ?
Will her soul abide
When her flesh hath died ?
The lyre is shattered, the music fled,
Her bosom is still, her soul is dead.

93

Say, thou heavenly sound,

Is thy being bound

By the broken lyre

Thou didst once inspire?

" Nay, in rolling spheres and in ocean's swell,

And in human heart of love I dwell."

And the soul replies,

" I gazed through those eyes,

And I warmed that cheek,

When I came to seek

For the deathless a dwelling in mortal clod ;

Now I go to the realm where I live in God."

THE RIVER

" From the great deep to the great deep he goes "

STREAM full fed by many a brooklet
  Babbling down to blend with thee,
Dancing, rushing, labouring onward
  To the unfathomed, boundless sea.

Mystic forces man ne'er measured,
  Out of darkness gave thee birth,
Past unknown and future hidden,
  Heaven-descended, born of Earth.

Out of ocean Heaven absorbed thee,
  Earth received thee, sent thee hither,
When or how or why we know not,
  Knowing thou returnest thither.

Out of darkness into darkness,

   Blind and borne by blinder Fate,

Rolling down a restless river,

   Child of Man, is this thy state?

If thy past be dim and voiceless

   And thy future fancy-wrought,

Let not either past or future

   Chafe thy soul with dubious thought. '

Like the gliding stream be happy

   In the life to-day possessed ;

Flowers rain upon its ripples,

   Bear them with thee, count thee blest.

While they bloom, enjoy them ; scorn them

   When they fade.   Is this enough?

Nay, our life is great and earnest

   And our conflict wild and rough.

Fling away this sensuous dreaming,
  Rise and battle in the van :
Work is waiting for the workers,
  Do for others what you can.

Like the swollen stream that borders
  All its banks with living green ;
This shall drown thy vague complaining
  For the shadowy in the seen.

Wherefore battle ? Wherefore labour ?
  Yet I am not satisfied.
Happy, all its life fulfilling,
  Sinks the stream in ocean's tide.

But my inmost soul is hungry
  For an individual breath ;
Whelmèd in a sea of being.
  Dying, 1 might well fear death.

7

All that earth can offer, leaves me
Wailing like an orphan lone ;
My unnumbered yearnings claim me,
God and Father, for Thine own.

Thou hast left, like skilful workman,
On Thy noblest work a mark ; *
Thou hast linked Divine and human ;
Light is ours from out the dark.

* One of the most notable sayings of Réné Descartes.

SUNSET

In Memoriam: Beatrice T——,

Died December 29th, 188—, Aged 27

Nay, leave it uncurtained, mother, that lingering
last red ray ;

I shall never behold it more, the light of God's
beautiful day.

And its evening comforts my spirit, that all
through its hours hath grieved

In grief for my half-lived life, in pangs for the
unachieved.

But now I am ready, mother ; let the passing bell
be rung,

For I go to-night, and the way is long, and I am
weak and young.

99

I need that good Christians should bow them in
prayer before God's throne

To win me strength for my journey, since I must
go alone.

The faces that I have looked on, I never shall see
again ;

The voices whose music I lived in, will speak to
my ear in vain.

Then tell me once more that He died and lay in
the grave for me,

And whisper His own sweet words, " I prepare a
place for thee " ;

That so, when the summons comes, and you watch
my ebbing breath,

I may trust myself in peace to the Lord of life and
death.

A LULLABY OF THE LAST SLEEP

Εἰ κεκοίμηται, σωθήσεται.—ST. JOHN xi. 12

WELL hast thou fought and borne and stood
  Well hast thou won the strife ;
Lie down beneath the holy rood,
  Loosed of the load of life.

Dream of the watch that angels keep,
  Dream that the night is past.
So gently, calmly, deeply sleep
  The sleep that is thy last.

No more shall weariness or pain
Conquer thy native fire ;
No more shall flesh and blood restrain
Thy spirit's high desire.

No more shall echoes loud and low
Rise till thy heart is riven.
From earth's unceasing cry of woe,
Reaching a righteous heaven.

No more shalt thou behold dismayed
Violence, greed and wrong,
Or error's myriad pitfalls laid
For all the heedless throng.

Rivers of peace around thee flow ;
Silence and endless rest
Refresh thy dull and aching brow,
And still thy heaving breast.

Body and mind alike repose,
All tumult banished hence,
When Death with kindly hand doth close
Each avenue of sense.

Thy spirit, yielded with thy breath,
Feeds its undazzled eyes
On thy throned Lord, who conquered Death,
At home in Paradise.

Till in Creation's springtide hour
He on thy rest shall shine,
And youth renewed in risen power,
Abundant life be thine.

MUTABLE AND IMMUTABLE

Ἵνα μείνῃ τὰ μὴ σαλευόμενα.—HEBREWS xii. 27

FLEETING, fleeting with the flying year,
Fleeting, fleeting fast,
All that our longing hearts hold dear—
Youth and strength and the buoyant breast,
Love and honour and gain and rest,
Till joy itself is past.

Fleeting, fleeting with the flying year,
Fleeting, fleeting fast,
All that our trembling spirits fear—
Eld and weakness and dulling care,
Loneness, reproach and dark despair,
Till pain itself is past.

Neither hath its abiding here ;

Hope, then fear, flies fast.

Whether of the twain abideth there ?

God will rule all, though man rebel,

And all He ruleth He loveth well.

So joy, not pain, shall last.

V

TALES OF THE NORTH

CORRIE-BHREACAN

A LEGEND OF THE WESTERN ISLES
OF SCOTLAND

FOAMING stream of Corrie-vreckan,
Chafing on the reef below,
Churning all the ocean hoary,
Snatching ships to whelming woe,

Swirling round, thy maddened billows
In the cauldron of the tide
Echo, as they spout and eddy,
Loud and clear, and far and wide :

" 'Mid the whirling wrecks of ages,
    This for ever standeth sure :
Man is strong as woman makes him
    Woman strong as she is pure ! "

Bhreacan, the heir of Lochlin,
    Reigned in every Danish heart,
Maidens shyly praised his prowess,
    Wished him well in field and mart.

For his princely mien was noble,
    And his princely eye was kind,
Mighty was his arm in battle,
    Dauntless was his royal mind.

Quoth the king, " My son, go wooing ;
    Bring thee home a Danish wife."
Bhreacan was free no longer,
    He had loved, and loved for life.

Not the blue-eyed Dane's fair tresses

   Braided smooth from neck to knee,

But a Highland girl's dark ringlets

   Bound him, as they fluttered free.

Far away swim misty islets

   That the monarch of the day,

Ere he sinks in boundless ocean,

   Kindles with a parting ray.

Fringing Scotia's coast, they render

   Homage to a haughty lord,

Father of the sweetest maiden

   Ardent lover e'er adored.

With the daring Dane he bargained :

   " Ere she doff her snood for thee,

Thou must anchor in the Whirlpool,

   Till the days and nights are three."

Denmark's sages met in council ;

Listened to the Prince's tale :

" I will win my love or perish ;

Tell me how I may prevail ! "

" Mighty ropes must hold the galley,

One for every day of test ;

Hemp the first, of wool the second,

While the third, the last and best,

" Must be woven from the tresses

Of the wearers of the snood ;

Then thou droppest anchor safely,

Through the might of maidenhood."

Bhreacan, the young and dauntless,

Had the love of Danish men ;

Danish maids, who shyly praised him,

Proved their deep devotion then.

For their long fair locks they gave him,
  Braided smooth from neck to knee ;
Then his galley, casting anchor,
  Rode upon the raging sea.

Shuddering like a hunted creature,
  She endured the billows' dash,
Though the hempen cable yielded,
  Sundering in a sudden crash.

When the second day was dawning,
  Burst the woollen rope in twain ;
But the tumult of the current
  Lashed the silky cord in vain.

Bhreacan had well-nigh won her
  Through the might of maidenhood ;
When the third day drew to evening,
  Still he faced the boiling flood.

8

Then the striving waves discovered
  One weak strand in all its length :
Feeblest link in any cable
  Is the measure of its strength.

One fair girl who shore her tresses
  Falsely bore a stainless name,
And relentless Corrie-vreckan
  Triumphed in her hidden shame.

Shattered was the trembling safeguard
  Reeled the ship in one fierce shock,
Then the hungry waters closing
  Sucked her to the fatal rock.

Watched the noble Highland maiden,
  Till the Viking's faithful hound
Dragged him from the waves, and laid him
  Dead beside her on the ground.

Plunging in again, he perished :

Then they piled his master's grave.

So she wore her snood for ever,

Finding none so true and brave.

Foaming stream of Corrie-vreckan,

Awful with a hero's doom,

Still thy rushing ferment echoes,

When the autumnal tempests boom :

" All our lives are linked together,

Like the Danish damsels' hair ;

To himself none liveth—others

In his life or death must share."

THE PASSING OF SCYLD

AN INCIDENT FROM "BEOWULF"

SCYLD is dead: the son of Scêf hath entered on the
fatal way;

Sorrow fills the hearts of all the warlike Danes
who owned his sway.

Bear him, comrades, ye who shared his deeds and
sat around his hearth,

Bear him on by naked heath and tangled holt and
well-tilled garth.

Never may we heap the pyre with helm and shield,
and lay thereon

Our loved lord, and light the bale-fire, so that men
when he is gone,

Faring o'er the paths of ocean, see his mound upon
the hill,

Call to mind his doughty doings, praise his matchless valour still.

Never can we build his barrow, tear by tear and
stone by stone,

For he willed to take his journey to the other land alone.

We have borne him from his mead-hall; nevermore
shall antlered roof

Echo to his footstep, never tremble to the trampling
hoof,

As he rides abroad to scatter all the scathers of our
race.

March we to the sandy sea-brim, to the fate-
appointed place.

Scyld is dead : the son of Scêf hath given up this
world for ever ;

But the Scyldings live, and nothing can his name
from Scyldings sever.

Sixty years ago he came to Denmark, none can
tell us whence ;

Sixty years have passed, and whither goeth now
our great defence ?

Sixty years ago the spoiler ravaged all our prince-
less land ;

Sixty years have passed, and now in health and
wealth and strength we stand.

Wisest Hunferth, with the snows of eighty winters
on thy brow,

Thou canst tell us all the story, when the champion
came and how.

" Watchers on the cliff were guarding Scedeland
from treacherous foe

Till the candle of the world was kindled, and its
golden glow

Spread o'er hill and dale and forest ; birds began
their morning hymn

As the rising sun discovered, partly bright and
partly dim,

Foamy-necked and birdlike flying o'er the flood,
a little skiff.

Treasure in its bosom glistened, when it nestled
'neath the cliff :

Writhen gold, and jewelled goblets shining like the
stars of heaven,

Necklaces for comely maidens, rings to chosen
heroes given,

Caskets brought from distant regions, heirloom
swords of tempered blade,

Burnished coats of mail whose meshes Weland
· Smith's own fingers made.

By the mast, amid the treasure, lay a rosy child
asleep,

All alone, a dimpled creature, cradled in the rock-
ing deep.

Grew to manhood's prime this Scêfing (he had
gained the mystic name,

Since we took him from the *ship's* deep bosom),
and he overcame

Hostile bands of many nations, who had made our
   land their prey,
Hail we him, great-hearted war-wolf, as our chief,
   and all obey
Far and wide, and bring their tribute, and he pays
   us for our toil,
Dealing from the royal gift-stool choicest treasure
   of the spoil.
So we do him service gladly, thronging round our noble
While the glee-beams at the banquet with the
   Scêfing's praises ring."

Scyld is dead : the son of Scêf hath chosen him the
   light of God ;
So we bring him to the shore that first his infant
   footsteps trod.
Waiteth there the lofty floater, with its ringed and
   twisted prow,
Outward bound and eager swaying on the curling
   breakers now.

'Tis the earl's enchanted ferry (never saw I fairer
skiff) ;

Treasure in its bosom glistens as it nestles 'neath
the cliff :

Writhen gold, and jewelled goblets shining like
the stars of heaven,

Necklaces for comely maidens, rings to chosen
heroes given,

Caskets brought from distant regions, heirloom
swords of tempered blade,

Burnished coats of mail whose meshes Weland
Smith's own fingers made.

By the mast, amid the treasure, place our dear and
aged lord ;

Lacks not one of all the number that whilom the
vessel stored.

O'er the cup of waves he journeys, in the keeping
of the flood ;

Set the gilded banner by him, groaning in your
mournful mood.

Let the shallow water waft him where the deep
sea-billows dance ;

Let the swan-road lead him on to ocean's measureless expanse.

Sixty years ago, athwart the dawn-lit mere his
bark drew nigh ;

Sixty years have passed, and now he sails beneath
the evening sky ;

Sixty years ago by Heaven this man was granted
to our prayer ;

Sixty years have passed, and he departeth into
God's own care.

Scyld is dead: the son of Scêf hath chosen the eternal g

Wan beneath the welkin stalking, Night hath
shadowed all the plain.

Who receives that freight, or where that vessel
anchors, none can tell ;

Whence and whither both are hidden ; but for
each, we know full well,

Better than a life of shame is death, which none

may hope to flee.

Sons of men, who dwell on earth, your narrow

couch made ready, see.

When the feast of life is finished, ye will sleep;

and it is best

That ye work while yet ye may, and pass from

worthy deeds to rest.

NOTE.—*See* " Beowulf," lines 1–52 ; 650–653; 1003–1009 ;
1192–1197; 1387–1390 ; 1802–1805; 2803–2809 ; 3138–3143 ;
3158–3164, etc., etc. I have translated literally many of its
characteristic periphrases, and have reproduced the religious in-
consistency due to its being a heathen saga, retouched by a
Christian editor.

VI

SONGS OF DEED AND DARING

THE KING OVER THE WATER

1746

HERE'S to the King that we longed for,

Sprung of our own royal race ;

Our fathers followed *his* fathers ;

Ours be not rebels' disgrace.

Southrons may bow to usurpers,

Dane, Norman, German, in turn ;

Hearts of his hunted adherents

Still for our sovereign yearn.

Here's to the King that we fought for,
　Sweeping the hireling swords
Over our marches, and chasing
　Them home to their panic-struck lords.
Bannockburn firing our courage,
　Tramped we through counties that quailed ;
Where were the men who should rally
　Till Charlie in England prevailed ?

Here's to the King that we bled for,
　Charging afresh o'er the killed,
Mown by the cowardly cannon,
　Drenching the soil we had tilled
With blood of the staunchest and boldest
　Who ever drew claymore, to flout
Dastardly, alien princeling,
　Smarting from Fontenoy's rout.

Here's to the King we are true to!

Stained with his grandfather's blood,

Driving his father to exile,

Pouring out gold in a flood,

Tempt they to basest of treasons,

Sale of his heir to our foes?

Breathes not a Scot who could barter

The Prince, or his refuge disclose.

Here's to the Cause we will live for,

Cause dearer still than the King.

Witness to Loyalty unswerving

On through the ages shall ring.

Tyrants may ravage our homesteads,

Rob us of garb and of name;

While we are leal men and brave men

Glory is ours, theirs is shame.

THE VOYAGE OF LIFE

THE stream is smooth, the wind is fair,

    Our little boat is fleet ;

My comrades, we are tired of toil

    And ease is passing sweet :

Then hoist the sail, fling by the oar,

    For gaily we will dream

While wind is warm and sun is kind,

    Drifting adown the stream.

The stream is smooth, the wind is fair—

    Stay ! Hark ! A rumbling roar,

The waters race towards the rocks,

    And down the gully pour.

Then ply the oar, and seize the helm,
    See how the foam-clouds gleam !
Haste ! haste ! and put the skiff about,
    And row against the stream.

Thus swiftly down the stream of Time
    Our heedless lives are borne ;
We fly from toil, and pain is shunned
    And duty laughed to scorn.
The stream is smooth and life is short,
    Then gaily let us dream ;
Be merry while we can, my boys,
    And travel with the stream.

'Tis easy drifting down the stream,
    Till breakers catch the craft ;
But only they will reach the port
    Who labour fore and aft.

Then ply the oar of stern resolve

That Right shall be supreme

To rule our days.   So help us God

To pull against the stream!

VII

TALES OF TO-DAY

THE SHEPHERD'S SUMMONS

A TRUE STORY

RELATED BY ONE OF THE CLERGY OF A WELL-KNOWN
ROMAN CATHOLIC CHURCH IN LONDON

AH! ye who do the business of the world
Know when and where ye work from day to day ;
But we, whom Holy Church hath given cure
Of her baptized children, oft are called
At times fixed by a wiser will than ours
To seek the lost sheep in the wilderness.

Once, as I waited for my penitents,
Charged with the message of forgiving love—
The last sweet canticle had soared to Heaven,
The altar lights burned low—there came to me

A woman, not to kneel unseen and pour

Confession, but to stand with summons clear :

" Your aid is sorely needed in a place

Where lies a young man now at point of death.

Come with me." And I answered, " In an hour ;

Till then my appointed ministry is here."

Her face was shadowed by her anxious thoughts,

Her clasped hands pleaded with her pleading voice :

" An hour ; and all the life to come at stake !

Haste, while you yet may guide his soul to God

In penitence and faith.   The time is short."

    And so she led me forth into the town,

Up one street, down another, on and on ;

And left me at the threshold of a house,

Questioning her who opened unto me.

I had been summoned to a dying man,

But youth and health were his who here abode.

Yet, strangely thither by a stranger led,

I lingered.   " Tell your master that a priest

Would fain speak with him on a weighty theme."

He gave me friendly greeting, and I urged
Christ's claim on all who bear His Holy Name,   .
On one who once had sought the means of grace
At my own hands ; but now for two whole years
Our worship had not wafted up his prayer,
So in the uncultured garden of that heart
Rank weeds of worldliness had grown apace.
Still, echoing the reproachful voice within,
My words found entrance ; and he owned his fault,
And thanked me that I cared for his true weal.

He could not tell me whence my summons came.
In vain I limned that gentle woman's face
In halting speech ; till, as I took my leave,
I saw it, imaged by the painter's art
And framed in pearls.   " Stay, this is she indeed,—
Your angel."   " 'Tis my mother you behold.
Ten years ago God took her saintly soul,
Or I had been a better Christian now.
Can her love watch, stronger than death, o'er me ?

At the tenth hour to-morrow I will come,

And make confession of my erring past."

My heart was full, I blessed him and withdrew,

Trusting his word so utterly that when

The tenth hour passed, and I was still alone,

I sought the unfolded sheep a second time.

The house was darkened.   He was slumbering still ;

Not to awaken till the Judgment Day.

Now take my tale, and spin your theories.

But let me still believe that she who came

From out the tomb—nay, rather from the light

Where God's dear saints pray for us—had been
     charged,

Through me, to seek one wanderer nigh to death,

By the Great Shepherd, Who once gave His life

For all the flock upon that bitter Cross.

EVORA

THRICE welcome ! With the holy Eastertide,
And with the earliest smile of tardy spring,
Thou comest, and I know how gladly, home.
But thou canst never know with what goodwill
My heart keeps holiday at thy return,
My own, my all, my daughter Evora.
Thrice welcome, for thy gentle childhood's sake,
And for thy dawning womanhood, which finds
Thee all thou wert and even more to me,
Now that the wandering sunshine of thy hair
Lies in a rope above thy broad white brow.
Thou standest 'mid the sprouting lilac trees,
Thy fresh cheek kindled with the year's first
    warmth,

Thy mantle fluttered by caressing winds,

Even as she stood there, seventeen years ago,

Who passed into the silence, leaving me

Deaf to the music of life's joy henceforth.

For her sake, welcome! With thy mother's form,

Thy mother's stature and thy mother's voice ;

Now thou art thus, she is not wholly dead.

She stood there smiling (thou hast her own smile),

My fair betrothed, whose wedding-day drew near.

But I had come to her with heavy news

Of sudden summons to the seat of war,

Where Britain's outposts waged a doubtful strife.

" I dare not claim thee for the dull suspense

That strains the patience of the soldier's wife."

" Think'st thou," she asked, "the circlet of pure
    gold

Could chain thy distant peril to my thoughts

More than this ruby's glow, this diamond's flash,

That sealed the vows which knit us soul to soul ? "

" I dare not bring thee home a partner maimed,

Whose helplessness might shadow all thy life."

" Give me the right to go and tend thee there.

Steel wounds not souls, and mars not therefore
    love,"

She answered, though she quivered as she spake.

" But steel may winnow out the deathless soul

From mortal frame, wherein we live and love ;

And Death hath many a dart that is not steel,

Where warriors suffer hardship in strange lands."

" My life must needs be widowed if thou fall,

Then let me mourn as one who bears thy name."

So we were joined and straightway sundered, ere

The flowers that made our bridal gay were dead.

Here as we parted that bright summer morn

We plucked, each for the other, one red rose

From yon south wall. I wore my fragrant
    bloom,

As dim devotion wears an amulet,

O'er sea and camp and battle-field, and still

Its faded petals cluster on their stem.

She laid hers in her bosom.   As we kissed

Once more, I murmured, " 'Twill not be for long

At Eastertide we surely meet again,

If God preserve me."   So I left her there ;

Yet turning saw the leaflets of her rose

Shower like rain upon her snowy robe.

The story of that winter hath been told

Elsewhere.   There were who fought and died

 unpraised,

There were who fought and lived and earned

 renown,

Till on a day the foe who seemed so strong

Fell utterly, and all the strife had end.

Then I outstript the news of my return,

And gained the village late on Easter Eve ;

Too late to cross the shadow-fretted fields

Under the glimmering moon and rouse the Hall.
" On Easter Day," I said, "we meet again."

But meanwhile sleep fled from my hungry eyes,
And daybreak led me forth and drew me on,
Rapt by the deep expectancy that stills
Hope, longing, love, vague fear, and whirling
    thought.
Scared at my step, one leveret dashed the dew
From yonder thicket, one melodious thrush
Prevented with her praise the myriad bells
That called men to adore the Risen Lord.
All else was hushed, and I was still drawn on,
On to her open window by the lawn.

I entered, as we enter God's own house,
And saw her sleeping in the pearly light,
And smiling as she slept ; her sunny hair
Strewn on the pillow like an aureole.
Her bosom seemed to heave, as if her dreams
Had lifted sin and sorrow from her soul

And borne it one brief hour to Paradise ;

And all the room was sweet with daffodils.

Yet something held me from her, and I stood,

How long I know not, gazing on her face,

And thanking God she was so passing fair.

" She will behold and greet me when she wakes,

Till morn is here I will not mar her rest."

But as the sunbeams shot into the room

Strange trembling came upon me, and my soul

Fainted to hear her voice.   When would the
    day

Unseal her lips ?   So reverently I bowed

O'er my beloved, and kissed an icy cheek.

I know no more, but that in this cold touch

I died to all, as all was dead to me,

All save thine orphaned wail, my Evora.

The daily turmoil of the world passed by

Unheeded and unheeding for a space,

Till I was summoned to my post again.

Then comrades told me time would heal my
 wound,
And when I answered, " I have lived my life,"
They gave me ampler pity than they give
To him who treads a solitary path
From dawn to eve ; or him who links his life
To one who cannot yield him love for love ;
Or him who woos ideal womanhood,
And, wedded, learns to call it but a dream.
The world accounts these happy when they die
With earth's best bliss untasted, life not lived.
But what are years of common, painless days
Of fame and ease, weighed with a single hour
Wherein one human soul entirely fair
Hath crowned our life's ideal with its love ?
My life *is* lived, and happier far is he
Who found and lost, than he who never finds.
The past is sweet, the future glows with hope ;
For she will see and know me when she wakes,
And we shall meet on Christ's great Easter Day.

10

"TILL DEATH US DO PART"

"Despairing of no man."—St. Luke vi. 35, R.V.

"THIS convict's wife is free to go and to share
with him his lot,

Or to stay behind and wed again, as if the
condemned were not."

My heart-throbs are like the steps of a fiend,
saying with mocking voice,

"Faithless wife or felon's wife, go, make thine
awful choice."

Echoes out of the days that are fled, echoes of
children at play,

Come thronging across my soul, "O Gaspar, you're
bad. I will go away,

And marry Eugene when I'm old enough, and not
be your little wife."

Eugene, upright like a rock at sea, lived his unswerving life ;

Gaspar was like the wave that smiles and plays in
the summer breeze,

Pleased with all that could pleasure afford, and
eager ever to please.

I gave a hand to each, as we roamed down the
blossomed paths of spring,

My flitting childish fancy to each dear comrade in
turn did cling.

To Eugene I went in my troubles, and leaned on
his strength for aid,

And valued his worth evermore, though sometimes
it made me afraid.

With Gaspar I laughed in my glee, until from his
light control

Some thwarted passion rushed into tempest and
darkened his soul.

Swiftly come, it was swiftly gone; and then he
would rue, not the storm,

But the check to our mirth and his, through the
storm-cloud's hideous form.

Years fled. Their boyish trebles passed into deep
tones of the man;

My childhood's bud was bursting out, and neigh-
bours were prompt to plan

Which should be first to pluck the petal that drank
the morning dew.

Not Eugene: his mien was changed, and quiet and
distant he grew:

He loved so deeply, he held his hand, lest he should
chance to spill

First dew from a cup that second dew could never
so sweetly fill.

But Gaspar sought me pleading: " Oh, would thou
wert ever at my side!

As brother and sister our paths diverge, then come
and be my bride."

I knew not my heart, nor his, nor the world ; I
    could not answer " Yes."
Then came the eager question again, and then the
    unguarded guess,
" 'Tis Eugene thou lov'st."   And then the girlish
    pique and flippant " No :
I shall not be good enough for him, however
    good I grow."
Yet he had made me dumb, with thought of good-
    ness without a taint.
Said Gaspar, " O far too good for me, who do not
    profess to be saint,
Whose heedless steps will lead me one day un-
    willing to some dread brink !
Beloved, thou canst save me, and only thou.   Save
    me, nor let me sink !
Say, wilt thou cling to the strong and make him
    glory more in his strength,
Or comfort the weak, who wanders else, on the
    toilsome journey's length ? "

Then the pitiful heart stirred in me, robbing of
will to withstand,
Made me woman ere he was man, and so I gave
him my hand.

That was May, and this is dull December in an icy
blast.
Stretched between them lay a summer-tide of hope
that could not last.
Not a wind to twist the bright-hued arras to the
other side
Where the tangles gather, where the devious
stitches straggle wide.
So my happiness in him drowned thought of doing
good to him ;
His the passions lulled, and his the humour un-
deformed by whim.
Heavenly Christ ! Thou saidst man's life consisteth
not in things possest ;
Rather, hew we out short cuts to death, and life
from living wrest,

While we toiling gather, while we vainly chase the
mocking pelf,

That returneth nevermore when wings it taketh to
itself.

Gaspar scattered gold uncounted ; made first
reckoning, when alarmed,

With a wily traitor who beneath a gala dress went
armed.

" As a friend, I counsel."   " Then I take advantage
of thee, friend."

So thro' meanest shifts and doublings, plunged in
darkness to the end,

End when he who thought to cozen, found himself
the only dupe.

" Ha, thou art silenced, O most cunning, O most
simple of our troop ! "

" Deed, not word, shall answer."   This the Southern
blood leapt up and roared,

And a grinning devil set a ready knife upon the
board.

I was going home to greet him, in my still un-
broken dream,

When a garrulous neighbour met me with an all-
absorbing theme :

How a newly welcomed traveller (little knew she
whom she told)

Proved himself the kindest friend to sick and poor,
to young and old ;

He had fondly loved a girl whom he could never
hope to gain ;

So he went to distant regions, lest perchance she
suffer pain

Knowing how he loved her. " Yet to me at least
'tis clear he knows,

Had he sought her, she had found him worthier
than the one she chose."

Worthier. Yes, Eugene ; and yet more blessed
has it been to give

To his need in Love's devotion than to hear thee
say " Receive."

Then my thoughts were sundered by the watchdog
as he sprang to greet

Steps that in the empty homestead news of " Wilful
murder " meet.

Humbled that the task I thought achieved had
never been begun,

Wounded that I knew not aught of all that he had
planned and done,

Mad with anguish, blindly then I rushed away, the
chain's whole length,

Which in happier days I felt not, save to triumph
in its strength ;

Now it well nigh strangled, as the blank and
miserable IS

Stood beside the WAS—the MAY BE, since the life,
no longer his—

God ! is sin so far away that any child of man
should look

As I looked upon that sinner, whom for weal or
woe I took ?

I relented not, until I heard the Law's stern voice
that said :

" Yes, his life is forfeit ; he ere long is numbered
with the dead."

Then one heartfelt cry went up, " God, spare him !"
And God hears the prayer ;

Death not yet, but death in life, where far away he
may outwear,

Outcast 'mid the outcasts, seasons measured by a
convict's toil,

While his doom, by law of God and man, unknits
the marriage coil.

Guiltless, I may break the union which availed
him not.   Alone

Be the doer of the deed, saith Justice, by the deed
undone.

As the tree falls, so it lies.   But why should my
fresh foliage be

Trampled in the mire because it clings about the
fallen tree ?

As it falls it lies, saith man. But what saith God
    in Heaven above?

"Of that fallen tree go make Me carvings for the
    place I love ;

Carvings that may stir devotion where, in holy
    mysteries,

Faithful people kneel to thank Me for My grace to
    such as these."

Fallen, lost, and ruined. Thou, who cam'st to seek
    and diedst to save,

In Thy love which hopeth all things, what are we
    that we should grave

This on tombstones none can roll away, entombing
    hopes of men ?

Since Thou bidst us share Thy work by giving, as
    Thou gavest then,

Not our words or alms, but even ourselves, that we
    may witness bear

Unto God's large pity, ever mightiest in man's
    despair ;

As the faithful moon that telleth of a glorious, changeless sun,

Shedding forth the light she borrows when his course unseen is run.

Hoping for this life, I gave ; and once upon Thine altar laid,

Hoping for a life beyond for him, I leave the debt once paid

At God's feet. I take the shame and exile, hearkening to His voice ;

Faithful wife and felon's wife ! So have I made my blessed choice.

NOTE.—The alternative described was actually, a few years since, put before a wife by a French court of law, who had given a murderer the benefit of "extenuating circumstances."

MY MIDNIGHT RIDE ON THE MOOR

THIS is the children's hour. Ye gather round
As day's brief light dies down ere lamps are lit
And fire-glows dance upon the glimmering walls,
To hear the old, new tale of what befel
Once, when I rode at night across the moor.

Picture me then a lad, but man enough
To love your gentle mother more than life.
Not yet I ventured whisper of my love,
Doubt left me hope that certainty might quench.
I was the stoutest lad the village held,
And owned the stoutest horse ; so could not choose
But go to seek the far-famed leech for her

Whom all the sorrowful had called their friend,

Whom all the poor had blessed for twenty years.

Holden of grievous sickness now she lay,

Racked by fierce pains that baffled all the lore

The wisest woman in the vale had gleaned.

(Women were ever wise in healing arts.)

But in the city dwelt the deftest hand,

The ablest brain, that ever gave their skill

To lessen human groans ; and two short hours

Might bring him in the morning to her side,

Drawn by the tireless steed with lungs of iron

That visited our village once a day,

Could one give news at sunrise of her need.

Evening drew on as I stroked Chieftain's neck,

Telling him why and whither we must wend,

And saddling him as I was wont to do.

So forth we paced beside the summer sea,

Rippling with joy beneath the sinking sun.

The golden clouds that kissed its laughing waves

Were not so golden as my love's young dreams :
Eventide's gentleness so wrought on me
That bounding hope sped with the fleetest barque,
And I could count her tenderest smile my own.

But as we turned away from the bright bay
Inland and eastward, rolling purple clouds
Dappled the sky.   I asked myself again,
" Why should the sweetest maid in all the world
Listen to me, when every man that breathes
Were fain to do her homage ? "   Then I chafed
That Chieftain's trot was blithe, till one faint star
Swam in the austere blue, and hid herself,
Like damsel coy, behind a mantling cloud.
When she stole forth upon the darkening heaven
My comfort came.   Better to feed the soul
With the far beauty of a lamp above,
Than grasp a rushlight honoured by my use !
Happiest he that wins, but happier they,
The few that loved, than all that never knew.

Yet my heart answered to the plaintive note

Sweeping along the tapering poles that run

Wirebound beside the road, and seem to grieve

For their lone nakedness, in sight of stems

Bowed by a quivering benison of leaves.

Day hears not such Æolian song as this,

Throbbing upon a silence only stirred

By Chieftain's speeding hoofs, and that sea-
mew

Who wails benighted far inland ; I see

Its wings flash past me in the strange star-
light,

Its cry hath echoes of a human woe.

Truly creation mourns with mourning man.

Mine is the only human heart that beats

On all this desolate land the plough contemns,

This moor where Autumn dons his royal robes,

Gold gorse and purple heather, mile on mile,

And Winter's dazzling raiment is unrent

From week to week upon the billowy meads.

Not so. O God, that was a woman's shriek !

That dim white fluttering is no sea-bird's wing,

But robe of anguished dame who succour needs.

Now, by my loyal love to one fair maid,

. All that an honest man may do, I dare !

Imagination mocks me—nought is here—

'Twas but the pitiful lone bird again.

The dizzy stars dance in a rising haze.

Brave Chieftain flags.   At midnight we must halt.

I know a hollow where a streamlet sings

And makes a pleasant greenness, canopied

By murmuring trees.   Here half our task is done.

Sleep drowns me in a moment as I sit.

And in my sleep I dream my love says " Nay,"

And shrieking flees across the shadowy moor.

Trembling I wake.   That shriek hath pierced
    beyond

The inner sense of which our dreams make sport.

11

For as I whistle Chieftain to my side

(He ne'er has harsher halter than my voice),

I find him near, and hungry for caress,

Thrusting a trembling face into my hand.

And as I draw the girth we hear once more

That weird lament and see that waving robe.

He plunges fear-struck ; and I search afresh

For the lorn wanderer, lavishing dear time,

Till the long road calls me to hasten on.

Mounting, I hear the voice beside my ear,

And know that she who cries is past my aid,

If not beyond God's mercy otherwhere.

Can I ride many a mile across the moor

With only that lost soul for company ?

My memory tells me of an inn that gives

Welcome of light and warmth and friendly voice

Half a mile hence, where I might wait for day.

And my desire goes out towards that inn,

Fleeing a doubtful wraith, and leaving thus

A living woman to the undoubtful chance

Of longer anguish and too tardy aid.

Cowardice, avaunt ! For duty's path ne'er led

To evil, though it often leads to pain.

So, urging Chieftain through the gathering gloom,

Past stunted trees waving deformèd arms,

Scourged by the harsh night wind, I meet wild
    rain,

Chill blast, and films of an unearthly garb

Flapping upon my face, and fiendish cries,

Dying in gibbering laughter, ring around.

Can I dare demons on a haunted moor ?

That by-path still leads quickly to the inn,

Welcome of light and warmth and friendly voice.

My blood stands still. Yet we unswerving strike

Down the defile that outworks the wide heath.

O'erhanging trees cling to its rocky sides

Which echo jingling rein and speeding hoof,

As anvil hammer ; all the straight white road

Is swallowed up in blackness; horrors press
Upon my brain; though seeing nought, I close
My eyes, as a scared child shuts out his fear,
Counting the footfalls, like one stunned from
    thought.
Till through my eyelids pierces sudden light.
Soft breezes fan me.   I behold, and lo,
A sheet of sunshine fallen upon the world.
Beyond that valley, day from night hath sprung,
And we have issued from the fearsome gloom
On morn's still radiance and the mounting lark.
The Minster bell floats o'er the dewy fields,
Summoning thus the newly-wakened town
To hallow a new week with Eucharist.

Well, children, I have told my lingering tale,
Living that night once more as I have told.
And now you ask me how my errand sped.
Came he in time?   And did she live?   One hour
Ago she took you in her kindly arms,

Garnering your story of the morning school.

For that long combat with my coward heart

Gave me ere long a mother and a wife.

The maid I loved had this response for me,

"Can I say 'Nay' to him who dared the moor,

With all its legends, for that dearest life?

Save for thy faith, I had been motherless."

And so her children call me father now.

What was the woful voice? That question seeks

An answer yet. Wind music, or a bird,

Delusion, or a dream, or living soul,

Or ghost uncomforted, or tempting fiend?

I know not. I have told you what I know.

But this I learned upon that awful night:

We wrestle not with flesh and blood alone.

What way the wicked hosts maintain their war

Is mystery; but howsoe'er they fight,

Their Conqueror is with us. I had fled,

Or flung away my reason on the moor,

Had not God heard my cry, and compassed me.

Perchance, I prayed 'gainst harms that are not
  harms,

That only borrow strength from our weak hearts;

Perchance, we heedless move 'mid greater harms;

God only knoweth what the darkness hides,

But light dwells with our Keeper evermore.

VIII

TWO VISIONS

DOLCE FAR NIENTE

WHIRR the swift clacking wheels above, around,
Morning and noonday and evening whirled
By the grim black engine with snorting sound.
In vain is the sunlight shed o'er the world ;
'Thwart that window the smoke hath always curled ;
And light would reveal, could it pierce the gloom,
Squalor and dust in that long, hot room.

Drive the senseless, ceaseless, resistless wheels
Dull gliding bands to and fro in the din,
Till to wan-cheeked children the whole room reels
God placed them His beautiful world within ;
Man must have workers his money to win ;
For living they labour till life is lost.
But is it worth earning at such a cost ?

From the toil, the heat, and the din I fled,

Saw the fading heavens, crimson and grey ;

The sunshine is dying, the day is dead.

Too soon hast thou left us, delightsome day,

Too soon is our youth all fleeting away.

Oh ! tarry a little longer, sweet light.

I fear the long hush of the chilly night.

Through gathering gloom I came down the hill,

And lay in the vale where the river rolled.

Dim in its darkening depths and still

The tall trees their nodding tops behold.

A faery boat with a rudder of gold

I saw, to a rugged trunk updrawn ;

I loosed it, and hastened to follow dawn.

Gently the waters bore me along,

Far over my head tree twined him with tree,

Till I heard the distant unceasing song,

The song of the boundless exultant sea.

I floated away on the ocean free,

Into the jewelled and wavering track

Where the fleecy clouds from the moon rolled back.

Then, swift as a thought or a bird's smooth wing,

Darted the boat through the path of light ;

Waves at her prow a long lullaby sing,

And hush me to sleep in the moonbeams white,

As a bird is hushed by approaching night.

Over my eyelids stole sleep's soft balm,

And thought drifted into a dreamless calm.

Her keel grated harsh on the shore propelled,

And I dreamed of a rending mountain grand ;

Till a ringing laugh all my dream dispelled,

And I saw the nymphs of a strange new land

Gleefully sport on the tawny sand,

Their ankles dewed by the circling sweep

Of the pearl-crowned waves that towards them creep.

They led me away to a shadowy nook,

Where the air was scented with orange bloom.

I dabbled my feet in a rippling brook,

They clad me in curious work of the loom,

Anointing my forehead with rich perfume ;

Then a twisted garland of white and blue

Faery flowers on my neck they threw.

Gaily we roamed down a mossy glade

Till we came to a gently rising ground,

And beheld a wide cool lawn displayed,

By tremulous birches belted round ;

There a banquet awaiting us we found,

And white-armed women, who bending bore

Dark water, and treasure of autumn's store.

The cloven pomegranate with ruby glow

On a crystal platter they gave me, and wine

Bubbling and sparkling they caused to flow

From a dewy goblet, and paused to twine
(While they bade me still on the grass recline)
Its silver margin with roses red,
And luscious grapes from the cluster shed.

We feasted and hearkened still to the notes
Of the throstle and bullfinch, who all the day
Poured torrents of song from their quivering throats.
Then a harp and a shining crown of bay,
To rejoice our hearts with a gladsome lay,
Were borne by a child with guileless eyes
To a dark-haired dame in a queenly guise.

Then she 'gan sing of that region blest
Where flowers never fade, where fruits never fail,
Where sunset glow cannot die in the west
Ere the car of Dawn in the east prevail,
And the lark responds to the nightingale ;
Where earth is as fair as the heaven above,
No strife for its peace, no tears in its love.

So they sang by turns.   When the final chord
Was struck, all the maidens rising flung
To each sweet singer a leafy reward.
They gave me the harp, and my heart's joy strung
Into music its strings, though I ne'er had sung.
And then they sprang up in their glee and beat
The tender turf with their glancing feet.

Thus I joyed with careless unbounded joy,
While the merry days all unheeded roll ;
Till all my delight began to cloy,
And the melting grape and the flower-crowned
    bowl
Nor refreshed my lips nor aroused my soul ;
And even the sonorous harp's sweet strain
Rang on in my ears with a sad refrain.

Oh, would that a withered leaf might fall
From the waving trees, or a sullen cloud
O'er the still blue heaven would drag its pall !

Or that I unthinking might laugh aloud

With the soulless nymphs who about me crowd !

Then into the deepest forest I rushed

Where 'neath tangled osiers a fountain gushed.

There the wind crept murmuring through the
     boughs

Whispering soft, " We can welcome morn

And spring when from winter and night they rouse ;

Oh, sunset is sweet to the labour-worn ! "

And the birds replied from the hoary thorn,

" Know the links of love are welded fast

By the burdens shared and the trials passed."

The grasshopper's " tettix " said in my ear,

" 'Tis for us who feed on the diamond dew,

Idly to chirrup the livelong year,

But work and its guerdon are given to you.

Then go, to your honoured lot be true."

While the dove in her secret recess alone

For a wailing and weary world made moan.

Oh, to find my magic bark and fly

Back to the world of work again !

I sank in the sands—they were ankle-high—

And the boat was drifting out on the main,

And the sky grew dark in a sudden rain.

With a cry, on the river's bank I woke

To hail the dark night and the city's smoke.

AMARANTH

" The idle singer of an empty day."

ON through the greatening city's gloomy streets

A Poet wandered ; round him roared and rolled

The ever-surging tide of human life.

Dim eyes met his from out the hurrying throng,

Hungry for higher blessing than they found

I' th' divers gains so eagerly pursued,

Which, like the mocking flame across the fen,

Fled as they followed, luring ever on

Through false morass to darkness and to death.

Sunk eyes met his of those who wrestled once

With fierce temptation, but were thrown, and now

The beast glares in a face once marked for God.

And faded women moved with weary feet,

Their souls so bowed by nameless, countless cares

They could not cast a glance to Heaven, a thought

On aught beyond their daily, dreary round ;

While little children at the corners swarmed,

Strewn like soiled blossoms from a spring-clad tree.

The Poet passed them by, and saw them not,

For all his soul was in his song, and all

His song was of the past ; so on he roamed,

Weaving a wreath of asphodel and thyme

And hyacinth to crown his brows, and struck

His lightly-twanging lyre, and gaily sang

Of the innumerous laugh of deathless gods,

Of white-armed nymphs at sport beneath the trees,

Of shepherds piping to their flocks, when yet

The world was young and men were full of mirth ;

He sang how knights of yore with vizor closed

Laid lance in rest to win themselves renown ;

How ladies fair in cauls of fretted gold

And ermined robes strolled on the castle leads,

To view their prowess and award the meed ;

In softer key he sang of sunny scenes

In Italy, of gliding gondolas,

Where dark-eyed dames lapt up in lanquid ease

Drew jewelled fingers through the waveless tide.

Most sweet, and all unheeded was the strain ;

No toil-worn brow relaxed ; but hastening on,

They marvelled on the lightness of his lay.

Two brawling, bare-armed women barred his road ;

A child clung quivering to the skirts of one,

Which, as he passed, fell on its face and sobbed,

And scattered all the cadence of a rime

Chanted beneath a moonlit balcony.

And then the Singer cried, " O jealous Fate,

To cast me on a world that has no room

For poets, that is sordid, deaf, and cold,

With downcast gaze and narrowing heart ; while I

Have worshipped all the beautiful in vain !

Ah ! times there were when round the ringing
   harp
Of the aged minstrel all the city thronged,
And wept and laughed to hear the tale he told.
And dimmer times there were when Orpheus drew
The lion from his prey, the tardy kine
From the meadow, and the pigeon from her mate,
And tamed the hearts of tigers with his song.
Such times are o'er ; farewell then, haunts of men,
For I will hence to Nature's solitude."

He sought the covert of the clustered copse ;
Where wind-swept branches bowed, like gracious
   dames,
Sweet greeting, and with wavering arms flung
   down
Long shadows flecked with light across the way.
There all was still, save when a crumpled leaf
Fell fluttering, or athwart the sunshine flashed
A frightened leveret wooing deeper shade.

And there he sang how upon summer eves

The vintage foams in overflowing vats ;

A song of mirth and careless jollity.

But all his voice died down in echo drear

And the reproachful murmur of the boughs.

He plunged in thicker gloom, where lofty elms

Shut daylight out and made of noon a night ;

Thin vapours slowly rose and all grew dim.

Onwards he strayed until the mist dissolved

Upon a dreamlike and unreal scene,

Such as blind mortals image forth the world

Of souls departed hence, when vagrant thought

Leaves all that is, to muse on what shall be.

A hollow sound of harping smote his ear,

Then he was in the middle of a group

Of those whose singing hath enriched the earth,

Teaching to men amid their daily toils

Theirs is a noble Whence and Whither still.

And all were chapleted with sacred bay,

Some had wide, leafy crowns half faded, some
But slender sprays that blossomed ever new,
And some had crowns that withered as he gazed.

And one there was, a faint yet kingly form,
His garland almost hid his clustering locks,
His keen eyes shone with changing light, his lip
Had felt and conquered all the shifts of fate.
The Singer did him reverence, and cried,
" O first and best of poets, who hast shrined
The world's heroic youth, and all ye bards,
Whose harps ring with the music of the past,
With classic chorus and with knightly rime,
Pity the warbler of untuneful days
That have nor theme nor ear to give to song."
" Son," the majestic minstrel smiling said,
" The times had been heroic when I lived,
But they were so no longer. Then I sang
Because my mind was troubled when I saw
Honour and hardy virtue all decayed

I pictured my Achilles, swift and strong,

And generous and dauntless, but the prey

Of fiercest passions uncontrolled, and thus

A lordly lion raging in his wrath,

Doomed to pull ruin on his friends, and fall

Untimely ere his purpose was achieved.

I sang ' the much enduring man,' who fled

Flowery Ogygia and the Scherian strand,

And pressed through stormy seas and savage realms,

At duty's call to rocky Ithaka."

Then from the shadowy crowd of forms well known,

And loved from childhood, clearer one face grew,

Eyes saddened with a heart-devouring grief,

Not because men gainsaid and banished him,

Nay, that great soul apart could never dwell,

Contented with its own sphere-harmonies,

While worlds were jangling discord in their woe.

Patient lips spoke : " Thou dreamest human hearts

'Neath glittering mail and tartaryne doublet beat

More noble than beneath your sombre vest.

Not so found I ; but seeing guile and hate

And selfish faction drag my Florence down,

I through the nine sad Circles of despair,

And up the Hill where souls are purified,

And into Light eternal mused my way ;

That I might tell how actions cannot end,

But wait for all their outcome till we pass

From the dim turmoil that we call our life."

Then one of ruddier hue and stronger voice,

He of the expanded brow and "ocean mind,"*

Came near, and grasped the Poet's hand : "Dost
     think

I wrote to tickle senseless ears, and fill

Vain eyes with merry sights, and chanced to please

More ages than I wrote for ?   Nay, around

I saw men jarring in their petty strifes,

Yet knew that deep in the immortal soul

Dwells harmony,† and so I strove to paint

---

* Coleridge, "Table Talk."   † *Merchant of Venice*, v. 1.

In mimic show man to his fellow-men.

Ye mock ; I wake your sympathy : ye hate ;

I bid you love : and pity, not despise."

" Well hast thou sung, O sweetest Shakespeare,"
   said

A clear, calm voice ; " but mine the nobler theme

And higher aim, though not so nearly reached.

I told men that God loved the world He made,

And plants again man's bartered Paradise.

But ere my soul was tuned to sing that song,

God made for me a peaceful solitude,

And shut out all the garish beams of day,

That I might bathe me in the light of Heaven."

The Poet saw, framed in long waving locks,

A placid brow and gentle lips, long since

Passed from their conflict into perfect peace.

Then like a wind that moans and swells and dies

About a lonely hillside cottage, rose

A mournful cry of many as of one :

" Oh, woe is me that when the sacred fire

Burned in my heart, I sang that I might please

The loiterers by the path of life, and strew

More scented blossoms in their dewy meads !

They had their hour's amusement, I my praise :

But now my garland fades, my name is dead,

And all my life is as it ne'er had been."

Thus far, and then the voice of drear com-
plaint

Was drowned in yet a louder wail of woe :

" I knew the heart of man was in my hand ;

I made his baser self prevail, and played

Passion's wild music, drove his shivering bark

Through boiling seas, and shipwrecked all his
life.

Now I would pass through agonies untold

To strangle out the life of my own words,

And tear this stinging garland from my brow."

Then as the clamour shrill and ceaseless grew,

And song and shriek and wail were madly blent
And round him closed weird forms with hopeless
eyes,
The Poet threw him on the earth and wept.

But lastly music conquered, and o'er all
The tumult thrilled a blissful harmony.
"O happy poets! who have spent yourselves
In mighty love for suffering fellow-men,
And poured out all your being in your song ;
Whose glorious voices sound thro' all the world,
Nerving the arm and comforting the heart,
And echoing on till time shall be no more ;
With poet's piercing eye and wingèd feet,
You climb the misty peaks of Truth, untouched
By human steps and rising nearest Heaven,
And there you kindle beacon-fires to guide
Men through waste moors, through forest, rock
and fen,
On, ever higher, to the final goal.

Though for a season poverty and scorn
Were yours; time tunes the hearts of men to hear,
And for the faithful singer garners up
A deathless name and amaranthine bay."*

* Κομεῖσθε τὸν ἀμαράντινον στέφανον.   1 Peter v. 4.

A Prize offered to the students of University College, London, in 1880, for the best English Composition upon "Thought and Action," was awarded to " Amaranth."

IX

HEBREW SKETCHES

MICHAL

I

" Michal, Saul's daughter, loved David "

LOST! From clinging arms and straining gaze my
    lord is fled and gone :
Blackest shadows by the moonbeam, blot him, as
    he hastens on,
From my father's whispering minions gathered
    round about our wall ;
Whom I balk thus of their prey, and brave the
    wrath of wrathful Saul.
Now I live upon those kisses till his lips are mine
    again,
Press my lips upon his pillow in the darkness, and
    see plain

David, all his face aglow while women pour the
joyous song :

" Saul slew thousands, David myriads, our champion true and strong."

So he bowed the hearts of all as one, that ruddy
shepherd lad.

All gave David praise and love, and two gave
everything they had :

Arms and fame and foremost station were my
brother's freewill gift,   .

And my heart leapt out like flame to him, though
scarce I dared to lift

Up my soul toward the height of being loved by
such as he ;

I, who thought it scorn to be the prize of any
victory,

Languished till my father kept his word, and
trembled when I knew

He would make my love abet his hate, " Let David
rise and do

Yet another deed, and he shall wed the daughter of
the king."

Hope and pride contended with my fears, and I
was fain to bring

Jacob's God a heartier prayer than I had ever
thought to pray.

"High the price you set upon her, higher still the
price I pay,"

Said my hero: "see your tale told twice; and all
the foes of God

Perish as these Gentile dogs whom I this day have
heaped with sod."

Ten score forfeit lives of Philistines made aliens
fear his name,

And our cloudless spring of love came following
hard upon his fame.

Hand in hand we sat beneath the stars, while
wandering breezes played

With thy harp strings, O my poet love, until my
whole soul swayed,

13

As the tide to moon, (so travellers tell) to that
sweet voice whose tone
Conquered Saul's dumb gloom, and all thy world of
love was mine alone ;
Though thy warrior feats and mounting thoughts
outsoared my baffled eyes.
So I crowned thee, David, king, I first, whose
quenchless star shall rise,
Borne from son-in-law to more than son, if sacred
oil can seal.
Hist ! weak woman, strong in wile through love, is
plotting for thy weal.
Yet I fear.   'Mid many fierce and crafty foes alone
he goes ;
" Yes, alone with God," he said, and smiled.   I
must believe he knows
That he loves that distant Being at whose voice I
cower and quake
When, in noonday hush, the woods in Gibeah with
His thunders shake ;

When He rides upon the storm, and grinds His
enemies to dust.

Him I dread, but to a human heart I give my
love and trust.

David's best-beloved of women needs no God else;
they may kill

Thee, they cannot slay our love; in life and death
I hold thee still.

II

"Michal despised David in her heart"

LOST! though thou art King of Israel, and Michal
is thy wife;

Lost! though all the foes are quelled who sought
the son of Jesse's life;

Not through Saul, but through Saul's fury boiling
in his daughter's blood.

Now my ire dies down, and unavailing tears come
like a flood;

Bitterer tears I shed not when my father tore me
  from our home,
Claimed by fond and foolish Phalti, who in earlier
  days had come
To be flouted by a reckless girl. My heart had
  broken then
Had not Jonathan, the bravest, gentlest, kindest
  among men,
Told me of my David's safety and unconquerable
  truth.
And I thought I had again the ardent lover of my
  youth,
When as crownèd king he sent for me, the daughter
  of the crushed.
All the untarnished love of Phalti's hapless captive
  forthwith gushed
Out to David only, as in happy maiden days of
  yore :
His the sealed and incensed shrine no other foot
  could e'er explore.

All I gave him once had then been his again, as
when he loved

Me alone. Alas! I found that pride and policy
had moved

Him to cleanse affront and place me, princess, on
the shepherd's throne.

Wily Abigail, the sot of Carmel's widow, for her
own

Held him now, with Jezreel's passionate Ahinoam,
who first

Made him father. David blindly loves that wanton
boy she nursed :

But I saw him snatch the morsel that they bore to
one who lay

Moaning in sore sickness. " Cost my toothsome
dainties what they may

To another, I will have them." That was written
on the face

Of the child. I saw him doomed to fall, a loathing
to his race,

In his prime, his mother's only grief she ever gave
    him birth.

And may God judge Abigail likewise by cutting off
    from earth

Pretty Daniel, proudly named by her who stole
    my husband's heart.

Stay! Such curses dull my pain, they cannot heal
    its cruel smart ;

Cannot win me back the lover whom my maddened
    words estranged ;

Cannot lay a babe upon my barren breast. How
    all is changed

Since I said, " God gave to Merab five fair sons
    and Adriel,

Me He dowered with David's love, so I most blest
    of women dwell."

All is changed since outraged love and wounded
    pride said words, not I,

Words of scorn for him I honoured most, when,
    kindled from on high,

Shone his zeal for the mysterious God, Whom
 lowlier now as king
Than whilom as shepherd lad he worships; while
 the people sing
He, like any starveling Levite, danced before that
 awful Ark.
My contempt was roused, and all the sky once lit
 by love grew dark,
For he answered scorn with scorn and told me of
 my father's fall.
Died then all his former tenderness for proud child
 of proud Saul.
Had I died before I said it! Nay, I said it, and I
 live
Widowed in the lifetime of my lord from all he
 once did give
When I first taught love's sweet lore to fresh and
 ardent heart to fan
Human love in him whom love for God made
 noblest son of man.

THE FIRE OF GOD.

A TALE TOLD BY JEDAIAH OF SAMARIA TO HIS SON, IN
THE DAYS OF JEHU, SON OF NIMSHI, KING OF
ISRAEL, IN THE FIRST YEAR OF HIS REIGN

CURSING again I curse them, for the Law

Doomed them to death six hundred years ago,

All those glib prophets, all those juggling priests,

Who throng our streets in their outlandish garb

Gathering to the solemn sacrifice

Which the new king proclaims. His hand still red

With Ahab's blood, he sins as Ahab sinned,

So may he die the death that Ahab died,

And his house perish like the house he slays.

Come thou, my foolish son, whom I have
plucked

From out the idol temple.   Dost thou ask

" Why should I not behold strange Baal's rites ? "

Wilt thou too join the multitude who say,

" At Dan and Bethel we will serve the God

Who brought us out of Egypt's cruel bonds ;

But in Samaria our prayers are made

To Baal, owned at Zidon and at Tyre,

That Israel may grow as wise as they,

The cunning with the trowel, oar, and loom.

Great is Jehovah.   Great is Baal too.

And both can bless and make their servants
        great."

Take heed, my son.   Ours is a jealous God,

Who will not share His glory.   This I learned

For ever, six-and-twenty years ago.

I followed Ahab through a fainting land,

Where two-and-forty months the dazzling sun

Had emptied all the storehouse of the deep.

The sky glowed like a furnace, and the flocks

That sought in hollows for the wonted springs

Finding nor herb nor water, panted forth

Their life upon the cracked and shrivelling ground ;

While men were mad with thirst, or quenching
    thirst

Perished of hunger on the barren soil.

Thus were the Sun-god's worshippers sore plagued

With drought and famine, while the foreign queen

Slaughtered the prophets of the Lord, whose voice

Had sealed the rain-clouds and dried up the dew.

Round the king's painted chariot thronged one
    day

Pale victims clamouring for the royal aid.

Forth from the melting crowd there strode one
    man,

Stern as his native rocks of Gilead,

With hair like Samson's on his shoulders tossed,

In sheepskin raiment of the pastoral tribes

Who scoff at our proud cities and rich plains,

Yet envy when they cross quick Jordan's flood.

Zeal for his God had kindled his fierce eyes,

And the king quailed before their wordless speech

More than before the raging Jezebel.

" Troubler of Israel, is it thou ? " he cried.

And the gaunt prophet said, " Not I, but thou

Hast troubled Israel.   Jehovah's Law

Thou didst forsake to follow Baalim."

    I thought to see the accuser mown to earth,

Or supplicated to remove his curse ;

Nay, Ahab cowered silent to receive

Commandment from the foe that he had banned :

" Gather thy people unto Carmel's Mount,

With all the seers of Baal and Asherah."

So, even as fish are swept into the net,

Israel gathered to the appointed place :

Where the bright waves lapped Carmel's ample

    skirts

East, north, and west, and Kishon's failing stream

Faltered with scarce a murmur to the deep.

All the thick woods that climb the mountain side

Languished in ruin round the crumbling pile

Built for an altar of our fathers' God.

Unbounded useless water mocked our thirst

On that side, and on this the pinnacles

Of Ahab's ivory house and idol fanes

Rose from the gardens of his fair Jezreel.

Here Baal's prophets marshalled their array,

Four hundred men and half a hundred more ;

Beside them were four hundred priests who taught

The shameful rites of Ashtoreth, and fed

From her most faithful votary's laden board.

Around them clustered Israel beguiled

By lies to leave God's truth, obedient

To the enthroned apostate in their midst.

And there the prophet of Jehovah stood,

One man alone, the one with whom was God.

Loud to the double-minded mob he cried,

" How long 'twixt two opinions will ye halt ?

Follow Jehovah if He be the God ;

If Baal, follow him." And all were dumb.

Then, kinglier than the king, he gave behest :

" Bring us two bullocks ; choose ye one and slay

And place it on the wood, and call your god ;

I will prepare the other in the name

Of mine ; and let him only be our God

Who fires the unkindled pile with flame divine."

So all was done according to his word.

The morn was breaking when they raised the cry,

" Hear, Baal ! " Louder song and swifter dance

Circled their untouched altar till high noon,

When the bold Tishbite held his peace no more,

But mocked their bootless folly. " Cry aloud !

Your god is musing ; he is at the chase ;

He journeys ; or he sleeps and must be waked.

Cry till he hears you, for he is a god."

At noon their chorus swelled, at noon they danced
Streaked with their own warm blood, till all the
    Mount
Rang with their frantic prayer and prophecy,
Their wild words wildly hurled to heaven, that fell
Unheeded back to earth.   The day declined :
Their cries grew fainter, and their weapons gleamed
More slowly, till they sank forspent to earth,
Their gaudy garments stained by desperate wounds.

And then Jehovah's prophet said, " Come near,"
And built the ruined altar of the Lord
With twelve great stones, a stone for every tribe,
And duly laid the sacrifice thereon ;
And all the trench about the altar filled
With water poured upon the offering thrice.
In Judah's Temple the unblemished lamb
Hallowed its evening worship when he spake
To Him who hears before the silent throng :
" Jehovah, Abram's, Isaac's, Jacob's God !

Let it be known this day that Thou art God
In Israel, that I Thy servant do
These things at Thy command. Hear me, O Lord,
That they may know that Thou art God indeed,
And that their wavering hearts are turned by
  Thee."
Then from the darkening evening sky there flashed
Fire which consumed the sacrifice, the wood,
The altar's stones and dust, and drained the
  trench,
Lapping the tide with which it brimmed erewhile.
Down on their faces all the people fell,
Shouting, " Jehovah, He is God alone ! "

Now His unheeded Law must be obeyed
Concerning those who lead our sons astray,
Ere earth could be refreshed and yield her fruits.
So at the prophet's word the people turned
On their blind guides and dragged them to the
  brook,

The ancient brook of Kishon, whose full flood
Once swelled to gulf the chariot and the horse
Of Sisera, and swept away our foes.
To-day its dusty bed was washed with blood.

Stern vengeance wrought, the awestruck host dis-
  persed ;
The man of God sought Carmel's loneliest height,
And prostrate pled for his repentant race.
Seven times he bade his servant go and gaze
Across the undimmed sky that spanned the sea ;
Till from the trembling sparkle floated up,
As thistledown drifts from its brilliant flower,
A cloudlet like the shadow of a hand.
It rode the air, still quivering with heat,
And summoned the dark squadrons of the sky.
They rushed together headlong o'er the blue ;
The forest bowed and groaned : the ocean swelled
In sudden tumult ; all the winds were loosed
From the four quarters of the earth, and all

The fountains of the deep were broken up.

From heaven's open windows God poured forth

Abundant blessing of long holden rain.

And so the curse was lifted from our land,

For one man's faith had turned a nation's heart.

Well was he named " Elijah " who proclaimed

That JAH alone is God.   His mission done,

He vanished as he came ; yet came again

Twice, once to Ahab, once to Ahab's son,

Since when we have not seen his dauntless face.

But no man knoweth of his sepulchre ;

Dim Sheol cannot claim him : nay, he passed

Deathless, like Enoch, unto God in Heaven,

Kept to restore our Israel some day,

And put away the idols God abhors.

I thought that day had come when Nimshi's son

Avenged the Lord of Ahab's house.   But lo!

He bids his subjects bow at Baal's shrine.

14

" Jehu shall serve him more than Ahab did."

Even now their riotous festival proceeds.

Hark !   But their shouts are shrieks, and mix with
    cries

Of men who vanquish and divide the spoil—

He traps them in their own iniquity !

So subtle is this strong, relentless king !

Towards the temple all the city streams ;

See, from its courts the royal guards have burst

With reddened blades ; they bear the idols forth,

Whose smoke mounts up, and the unholy house

Sinks crashing on the dying and the dead.

Fallen is Baal, ne'er again to rise.

Praise to the Lord, our King for evermore.

X

SONGS OF THE SEEN AND UNSEEN

MAY DAWN

HARK ! from the spring-gladdened tree
    Singeth the merle,
Singeth to God, awakening thee.
Rise, poet, rise and see
    Morning unfurl.
Winter has long held sway,
    Chill was the night ;
Dawn glory drives the clouds away,
Hope, on the rosy wings of day,
    Riseth in light.
God giveth youth and dawn and spring,
    Life lies before us ;
Birds soar on dewy wing,
    Swelling the chorus ;

While the sun triumphing,
   Flames through his portal
Rise, poet, rise and sing,
   "Man is immortal."

IN AN AVENUE

On, where the saplings shoot
Yet in their young joy mute :
   To the tender feet
   Is the moss most sweet;
And the rich-breath'd violets root.

On, where the tall trunks spring,
And arms to heaven upfling,
   In the new delight
   Of the coming might ;
While birds in their branches sing.

On, where the stately trees
Sway slowly in the breeze,

In calm strength endued
Once again renewed ;
They cradle the nests at ease.

On, where giants across the heath
Stretch gaunt arms in living death.
    Left in that grim clutch
    'Spite of Spring's soft touch ;
With a stony ground beneath.

Fair Avilion stands ajar,
Cloudy pillar, crimson bar,
    Through whose portals dim
    Shadowy beings swim
Into seas of light that are near and far.

On—but thither no path brings
Souls borne down by earthly things.
    So we gaze and cry
    To the glowing sky,
" O God, give strength to our wings."

VOICELESS

Music hath murmured round my ears,
  Hath held me by enchantment strong,
And I have been from childhood's years
  Haunted by sweetest song.
I soared, desiring still to see
  The invisible, that purest flame
Of primal orbs might lighten me ;
  But utterance never came.
The silence filled my soul with pain.
  I cried to Nature, bade her tell
To me her secret ; all in vain :
  And yet I loved her well.

At dawn upon the first of May

    Woodward I went for aid to seek ;

My quickened heart had much to say,

    But still I could not speak.

Dame Nature held her court anon,

    The herald cuckoo summons sang,

The trees their fresh attire put on,

    Flowers at her footstool sprang.

The birds were quiring all at once,

    " Gloria Patri " loud and low ;

My lips took up the glad response,

    " Gloria Filio."

Ye heavenly birds, your anthems made

    In higher air unbidden come—

I paused, for on the hawthorn swayed

    One new-fledged throstle dumb.

And I was dumb.   I heard his note

    Complaining, " At my heart's request

I sang, and ceased with throbbing throat,

    Tired limbs, and ruffled breast.

Wherefore ?   Because the day was bright,

   And Spring had come to bless the earth,

The darkness had been quelled by light

   And morn again had birth.

Hath not the day been always bright ?

   Is not the earth for ever young ?

Hath not the triumph of the light

   Ten thousand times been sung ?

Go, trivial warblers, tune your lays,

   And thrill with well-worn themes the air.

I wait a subject of my praise

   In something new and rare."

Now while he spake a shuddering went

   Through all the wood foretelling shower,

The trees upon each other leant,

   Dull did the welkin lower.

Then all the songs are hushed and all

   The flowers bow their heads and close ;

And fast and fierce the waters fall,

   And shrill the tempest blows.

That throstle, when the storm was o'er

And rainbow smiles dispelled the wrath,

Crept from the dripping leaves to pour

A heart-wrought music forth.

From him I learned that there are chords

No passing idle zephyrs sweep—

The tempest only wakes in words

Their voices strong and deep.

TRUE ART

Η μνήμη πρὸς τὴν τοῦ κάλλους φύσιν ἣν ἐχθη, καὶ πάλιν ἐῖδεν αυτὴν
μετὰ σωφροσύνης ἐν ἀγνῷ βάθρῳ βεβῶσαν.—PLATO.

LOVE thou the Beautiful like some bright flower
That climbs about the hillside steep and bare,
Unseen of any human eye, to shower
Her wealth of form and hue and fragrance there,
As o'er the rock her tracery she flings ;
Or like the lark that solitary sings ;
Strive, heedless of reward, to make the world more
    fair.

Love thou the Beautiful with self-less love,
Mute veneration, and a soul athirst
For the Beyond.   Soar like a bird above

These vanities, where men in mists immersed

Are babbling in the dark what names to call

The shadows flickering on their prison wall.

Despise thou them, but spread thy folded pinions

    first.

Love thou the Beautiful till it unveil

Itself unto the heart that can adore,

In starlit midnight seas where foam-lines frail

Tremble in light along the echoing shore ;

Or dancing sunlit corn, or mountain peak

Rising from out its cloud-zone heaven to seek ;

Or in the mingling music winds and waters roar.

In silence of thine heart-subduing awe

Glimpses of things unearthly flash on thee.

They are but slanting sun-rays sent to draw

Thy heaven-descended soul, that pined to be

In clearer air, up to the unseen, fair

Realm of the Real.   Thou transplanted there

Discerning the true Beautiful, the false shalt flee.

For know that all the Beautiful is true :

And all the True is fair, and all the Good

Is beautiful and true.   Thus ever new

Yet ever old, the immortal triad stood.

Truth, goodness, with unloveliness combined,

Base and yet beautiful we cannot find :

Nature hath no such wayward discord in her

    mood

UNTO THE HILLS

"Nature is the Art of God."—SIR THOMAS BROWNE's "Religio
Medici," sect. 16.

As man from dull pursuit of petty ends,

Or vexings manifold of worldly care,

Looks up at times and drinks the morning breeze,

He knows his little life is like a road

Lighted some short space by a flickering glare

And drowned in darkness of a vast Beyond.

Unsatisfied in spirit, then he seeks

To utter all his longing for a life

Larger and fuller than his life to-day.

He moulds and paints things fairer than he knows,

He piles mute stones to point unto the sky,

He pours out his ascending thought in song,

Or, if it baffle speech, he lets it forth

In maiden music words can never wed

To which our heartstrings vibrate one by one.

And thus he half unveils his mind in Art,

Not wholly ; for he knows not all he is,

Nor can the artist fathom his own work.

So likewise God unveils His mind divine

In Art Divine ; not wholly, though His works

Are all known to Him since the world began,

But even as men may bear the epiphany.

Nature is God's Art, where He moulds and paints

And builds, and poesy and music makes,

That whosoever will may learn of Him.

In crowded vales, where fog-wreaths hang, we lose

Our sense of an encompassing Unseen,

Our yearning for a higher life in God ;

Our souls grow like the turbid, stagnant pool,

Where worthless remnants float 'mid choking

  weeds.

15

But here the everlasting hills can teach

The open eye and understanding soul.

" Lift up your hearts," their soaring summits cry,

" Lift up your hearts, and let your souls reflect

The image ye were made in, as the lake

Receives the image of her brooding hills

Dark with the sullen storm-cloud, scarred and
    bare,

Or laughing in the sunlight and aglow

In ruddy heather blent with vivid green."

Hills, ere ye melt into the dusky sky,

After a radiant eventide hath clothed

With rare pink hues your rugged sides whereon

The shadows of the unlit peaks repose,

Tell us that God is strong, though we are weak ;

And that He changeth not, although we change ;

And stay our souls on His eternity.

Ye vanish ; and we leave your calm abodes,

Striving to keep the mirror of our soul

Unruffled, lest we earn that old rebuke

To Syria, fighting God who made the hills

In valleys, where she owned not that He reigned.

God of the Hills, who didst Thyself reveal

In thunder-clouds on Sinai's awful brow ;

Who on a mount didst set Thy chosen king,

And enteredst as the King of Glory there ;

Till on Moriah rose for Thine abode

In holy beauty that great House of Prayer ;

God of the Hills, who gavest Thy New Law,

Hiding Thyself in flesh, upon a mount

Washed by the smiling wave of Galilee ;

Who didst unveil Thy majesty divine

Where Hermon rears his crest of untrod snow ;

And who from Olivet wast taken up

To claim Thy royal seat in Heaven, until

On Olivet the earth shall own Thee King ;

God of the Hills, make these, the noblest works

In Thy great Art of Nature, unto us

A glorious apocalypse of Thee !

DERWENTWATER, *August*, 1887.

TO A KINGFISHER

" Omnia exeunt in mysterium."

WHENCE and whither,

Halcyon of varied hue,

Who camest hither

Robed in Heaven's own blue,

Like a flash of light

From the sedges' night

To our 'wildered sight,

With thy sapphire wing

And thy jacinth breast?

Where, oh, where,

O thought-swift thing

From the upper air,

Hast thou made thy nest

And set up thy rest?

Did thy charming song

Soothe the ocean's rage,

And its waves engage

To sing lullaby

To a cloudless sky

And thy callow young?

    Away! Away!

Like arrow from bow,

In thy gladsome play,

Whither, none may know.

We may reckon the rushes whence thou hast fled,

We may weigh the brain, we may map the head;

But the bird is gone through the trackless glen,

And the kingdom of thought is beyond our ken.

Fair is the shimmering lake in whose cool glass

The wide, clear heaven beholds his face and

    smiles;

And sweetly cluster on the tender grass

The birches' silvery shafts in long defiles;

Beside the brimming river

They stand and shiver,

As waiting to be clothed upon when Spring

The life-chime of her Easter bells doth ring.

Not fairer than before thou cam'st, bright bird,

And yet more fair to me.

For then the open page lay dim and blurred,

An unknown tongue, scarce heard

Nor vaguely understood,

On which God's finger wrote that all might see,

" 'Tis beautiful and good."

Thou wert the informing spirit of the whole,

Unveiling to my soul its soul.

For Nature's stillness had no speech

Which could avail that soul to reach.

'Twas Life without that met with Life within,

Two deep notes merging into one full chord,

Two tapers flashing into one white flame,

That lit up all, and made its music win

Upon my ear, and all the sweetness stored

Became to me the same, yet not the same.

For Life is motion, scanned and searched and
tried,

Since all things change, and in their change
abide.

Life is the touch of God, nay, rather say,

'Tis God Himself, who works in wondrous
way.

Such words may place a crown

On Science' brow at will

Of realms unconquered still,

Where Nescience holds her own.

But Life we know and know not,

Give and give not, take and take not;

Its origin we show not

And power of Nescience shake not.

And Nature crowns the gifts that man receives,

Through Life unriddling for us what she gives.

So by her guidance kind

We rise from sense to mind;

Until she points to realms beyond

Through which she cannot lead.

Then reasonings dim and fancies fond

And fitful feelings need

Strong wings of Love, to bear them to the sun.

A human face must shine

With all we call Divine ;

A human heart must beat that we have won.

More than all the sages' store

Life can teach us Nature's lore :

Paths that knowledge never trod

Lead through human Love to God.

VIRGINIA WATER, *March*, 1885.

LIFE'S DAWNING

THE gladsome Christmas Day drew on apace,
And from the great Cathedral dedicate
To the most highly favoured of her race
Deep bells were pealing through the midnight frost,
Hailing One born the Heir of all the worlds.

Their joy found echo in a woman's soul
With first faint whisper of ecstatic hope,
" The crowning bliss of motherhood shall be
Thine own, and thou shalt bear a child to him
Who stands beside thee, owning all thy love."

Even at that hour a new life had begun,
Dawning from darkness as the daylight dawns

None can say when ; a human soul then lived

For Him to whom all live.   But she who took

That gift from God could scarcely say 'twas given

With that dim promise, or with growing hope,

With secret flutterings of the coming pulse,

Or throb of the new heart-beat at her heart,

As the babe grew, expecting light and love ;

Or when in anguish that becometh joy

Beyond all joy, she bowed herself, and heard

The cry with which he drank the breath of life

And saw the sunshine first ; or when her arms

Clasped him to all her bosom's warmth, while he,

Taking uncertain hold on mortal life,

Waked but to sleep again, and scarce unclosed

His languid eyes, and stirred not as he lay,

And her life nourished his from hour to hour ;

Or when from week to week the infant changed

To child, and child to lad, and lad to man ;

Smiled to behold her, clung to her embrace,

Knew her for " mother " out of all the world ;

Laboured for her and bade her lean on him,

And made the strength and sunshine of her days.

Yet thus enriched the mother cannot say,

" At such an hour my son was given to me."

Birth is but one link in the chain of life.

I woke from unremembered dreaming then

To life that holds no place in memory

Till months have grown to years ; and slowly came

To know my world, my fellows, and myself.

What Birth began not, cannot end with death.

From this dim, prisoned dream I shall awake

To know the Life Indeed, and to become

At last what God foresaw His child should prove,

When from the void He summoned me to be.

XI

CHRISTIAN SKETCHES

THE BLESSED MOTHER

THIRTY-FOUR years ago, when all our towns
Were pouring forth their sons upon the road
That led them up to Zion for the Feast,
I, a betrothed maid, was left one eve
Alone beside the well at Nazareth.
Home from the water-drawing all the rest
Had gone ; their converse in the distance died,
While I mused many things, and saw my life
Lived out like all the lives among our hills
In homely duties to my spouse and God.
When lo ! the fading glory of the west
Brightened anew, and forth to me there came
An angel, awful with the light of Heaven,
Who brought more awful tidings. I should be

The virgin mother of the Son of God ;

Messiah, David's heir, should be my Son ;

I, sinful, yet should bear a sinless Birth.

Hath earth a draught of sorrow deep enough

To quench the joy of such a motherhood ?

It hath, for, I have seen my heavenly Son,

The Holy One whom I a maiden bore,

Mocked and despised by those He came to save,

Haled as a felon to the Hill of Shame,

Nailed to the anguish of the Roman cross,

Scorned, outcast, and forsaken of His friends.

When to His bleeding feet I crept, the sword

Pierced through and through me as the seer foretold.

He saw me, He who leaned upon my love

In childhood, and on whose strong love I leaned,

The widowed mother of an only Son,

Through years of lowly toil and patient trust.

He saw me claim my Son unto the end,

And Mary, whom the seven demons thralled,

Still own Him Saviour, and His kinsman John

Whom He loved even as David Jonathan,

The only true one of His chosen band,

Stand there amid the women 'neath His cross.

The wife of Clopas and the Magdalene

Blinded their eyes with weeping sore, but I

Gazed tearless on the torture of my Son,

Longing to die when He gave up the ghost.

He saw me ; with the death-dews on His brow

He thought upon my sorrow.   There is room

For every human grief within the heart

That kept no corner for its own desire,

No private nook to brood on its own pain.

Pitying all, He pitied not Himself,

Saving the world from everlasting woe,

And loving all by loving each, He saved

Me from the madness of that dumb despair.

16

So, yet more tenderly than when He calmed

My sobs as Joseph died, He said to me,

" Woman, behold thy son."   And then to John,

" Behold thy mother."   Thus He forged that hour

The first of all those countless links of love

That bind to one another all whom faith

Binds to Him till the ending of the age.

Then His disciple led me down the Hill

Of Golgotha, and we two wait in prayer

Until the blackness of that guilty noon

Yield to the brightness of a fadeless morn

When He shall rise again, as He foretold,

Who spoke the wholly truthful words of God.

HERMON

" 'Εποπται γενηθέντες τῆς ἐκείνου μεγαλειότητος."—2 Peter i. 16

FROM out the orient sky's deep amethyst

The myriad eyes of heaven gaze one by one ;

And Nature, like a child with wailing spent,

Lies slumbering ; all the burden and the heat

That morning brought hath vanished with the day.

Great Hermon's crown of snow, which lately rose

Flushed by the kisses of the setting sun,

Flings the reflection of a paler orb

In mantling moonbeams o'er his bristling crags

And fathomless ravines ; and far below

His dewy slopes and girdling vineyards sleep.

Beyond this aged Sheikh of all the hills *

* Jebel-esh-Sheikh, modern name of Hermon.

Lebanon's rugged ridges stretch away

Toward the darkening north.   Far on the east,

'Twixt fertilising streams of high renown,

White-roofed Damascus dreams amid her broad

Well-watered gardens and encircling hills.

And clinging to the mountain's southern skirts

Ancient Paneas * in a reedy plain

Her marble temple rears, with grots and groves

Which Canaan's Baal yields to Grecian Pan.

In whose grim caverns Jordan's swelling source

Bursts from the earth with overwhelming might,

And roaring rushes thro' his rocky bed

On to Esdraëlon's luxuriant fields,

The battle-ground and garden of the land.

While in the region that receives the sun

The Tideless Sea is strewn with twinkling waves.

Four travellers, thro' the twilight toiling up,

Have gained a lonely height of Hermon's pile ;

* Cæsarea Philippi, formerly Baal-gad.

Wrapped in their long striped abbas three sink
  down
Heavy with slumber on the rocky ground,
Sorely perplexed, for through their loyal souls
Words of deep awe and dread import have swept
Echoing for six long days of still suspense,
" This is Messiah, King of Israel,
The true Messiah who is the Son of God."
And while they thus in exultation learn
The coming triumph of this Son of God,
Unveiling of a deeper mystery
Baffles their hopes, and wrings their hearts with
  woe :
" The Son of Man must suffer many things,
And must be killed, and rise again."   And then
Comes a first whisper of the accursed cross,
The slave's last terror and the felon's doom.
No wonder they are awed and sore perplexed,
Seeing their Master kneeling there with God,
Who led them up that mountain side to pray :

Yet they are overcome with drowsy sleep ;
And He, toilworn, is watching still for ease
Hath no allurements, while the sheep He seeks
Unshepherded, unpastured, roam around.
The unquiet night-wind moans, and still He kneels,
A wandering suppliant on the earth He made,
Till solemn midnight hushes all the land.

Then fully wakened from their fitful watch
The faithful, honoured, and bewildered three
Behold a vision as of Paradise,
While yet on earth, for every star has paled,
Yon glistening crest is dimmed ; and Nature's
 King—
Whose is the strength of all the hills, whose hand
Creates and guides the stars—is crowned of God
With majesty and might. His raiment shines
More dazzling than the snow that gleams above,
His countenance is as the sun, and thus
He clothes Himself with light as very God.

And standing glorified with Him appear

His great forerunners, leaders of the band

Of witnesses to all the Law fulfilled

By yet a greater Prophet, who like them

Hath fasted forty days and forty nights.

Awe-struck, with Him they speak, those wondrous
    guests,

Who mightily endowed with Death had striven,

Had dared him in the service of the Lord,

Had launched his arrows o'er an impious land,

And torn his victims from his greedy grasp :

Till when their summons from this life rang
    out

Chariots of Heaven and archangelic strength

Bore from the baffled spoiler all his prey.

They speak of greater triumphs : of the Christ

Contending with the foe ; of His decease,

His going forth into the realm of shades

To rob it of its terrors, and return

With Death a captive at His conquering wheels.

Dazed with the glory of the Holy Mount,

Whereon the true Shechînah's beams descend

The apostles stand : till, gliding from their gaze,

Those saintly seers depart.   Then Peter cries :—

" Rabbi, 'tis good for us that we abide.

Here, if Thou wilt, three leafy tents we raise

For Thee, for Moses, and Elias, Lord."

Thus crazed with fear he knows not what to say.

But even while he speaks, a radiant cloud

O'ershadows them, and hides Him with its light,

And round them trembling draws its misty skirts ;

And from the cloud an awe-compelling voice,

" Lo ! this is my beloved Son, whom I

Have chosen,* and in whom I am well pleased.

Hear Him."   JEHOVAH'S well-beloved Son,

Who called no man His father, who was deemed

Unworthy to be son of Israël ;

Chosen of God, whom all the world rejects ;

Pleasing to God, who all mankind offends.

* Vatican and Sinaitic MSS.

Their awe has deepened into direst fear,

And even as Moses and the Tishbite stern

Once hid their faces from the Lord of Hosts,

They prostrate fall.

A hand is laid upon them, and a voice—

Of mother's tenderness and monarch's strength,

That children loved, that demons quailed to hear,

That made the storm a calm, that raised the dead—

Soothes all their troubled spirits with a word :

" Arise. Fear not." Uplifting then their eyes,

They look around, but no man met their gaze

Save Jesus only, Jesus with themselves,

The Christ whom they believed, adored, and
    served ;

The same who shared their humble daily life,

The same whose royal glory was revealed,

The same in weakness and in agony,

The same who reigns and intercedes above,

Yesterday, now, eternally the same.

The sky is streaked with dawning light, and down

That mountain's side in converse sweet they
wend ;

And still the glory rests upon His brow

That consecrates Him as the Lamb of God

Who gave Himself and was so freely given

To bear the sin of all the world away:

Great Victim crowned with light ! but man (whose
need

Of Thee has groaned thro' each succeeding age)

Weaves Thee no garland, save of thorns ; nor finds

A nobler altar than the tree of shame ;

Nor worthier priests to shed Thy sacred blood

Than brutal Roman soldiers, who to Thee

Pour for libation vinegar and gall ;

Their sacrificial pæan frantic taunts,

And curses by the accursed rabble howled.

Now at this crisis once more set apart

By the same heavenly Oracle that first

Thrilled thro' the wintry sky o'er Jordan's flood

When at Thy baptism Thy work began ;

That shall 'mid rolling thunders sound again,*

When Sadducee and Pharisee and Scribe

Despise, reject, conspire against their King,

And scorn the blessings of the Sent of God ;

When Hell shall furbish all her arms, and drive

Her legions forth in hideous array ;

And angel songs are silenced as there falls

Athwart Thy path the shadow of the Cross.

The sun has risen on another day.

At Hermon's base the patient Saviour stands,

Amid the sinful, suffering, toiling world,

While wondering multitudes who meet Him there

Down at His feet in adoration fall.

* John xii. 28.

NOTE.—The weight of modern evidence is in favour of one of the spurs of Hermon as the scene of the Transfiguration. Tabor, the traditional scene, was at that time crowned by a fortress. The mention of the disciples being overcome with sleep, the numerous instances of our Lord passing nights in solitary prayer on a mountain, and the fact that the lunatic child was healed "on the next day," all lead us to infer that it took place at night.

SAINT CATHARINE OF EGYPT

MARTYRED NOVEMBER 25TH, A.D. 307

THERE is a tomb upon a sacred mount
At Sinai ; where angry clouds once met
In shock of strife, and Heaven's cannonade
Shook earth, and Israel all trembling heard
Far from the restless stir of this mad world,
The voice of JAHVEH in the Wilderness.
Here Jebel-Musa altar-like lifts up
Its rugged head ; and to its neighbour peak—
Known henceforth as the Jebel-Katherin—
A flight of angels bore the holy dead,
Saint Catharine the Virgin, royal, fair,
Wise, true, and steadfast, who was wholly Christ's.
And after many hundred years they found

Her sleeping there, with raiment waxen old,

And wealth of tresses wrapping her around

Like gleaming robe of Ind ; and radiance shone

Upon her brow, and fragrance filled the tomb.

'Tis thus they tell the story of her life.

Costis and Sabinella, King and Queen,

Ruled Egypt, and were parents passing rich

Though God had given them but a maiden babe.

For she was fairer than an April day,

And wiser than the sages of old time.

While other damsels with their trinkets toyed,

Dreaming of lovers in the days to come,

She, cradled in the Land of Light, the land

The sun loves best of all he looks upon,

The land where stars make night a softer day,

And the chaste moon seems most adorable,

Climbed to the lofty tower Costis built,

And searched the heavens with wonder and
    delight ;

Or turned to her beloved Athenian scrolls,

And, borne in fiery chariot of high thought,

Saw things eternal, reaching what we were

And what we might be were the soul set free,

Till pomps and gauds of earth grew lustreless

While she could sit alone at Plato's feet.

Ere early youth was spent her parents' crown

Weighted her delicate white brow; then came

Her people, praying she would mate with one

Able to share her rule and lead them forth

To victory ; and she was sore perplexed.

" But who is he that I must wed ? " she cried.

" O sovereign Lady, our dear dread, your gifts

Are manifold ; so heed our loving plea.

And for that you are sprung of noble race,

And for that you are heir of this great realm,

And for that you are wisest of mankind,

And for that you are fairest of all flesh,

Bless some great noble with your plighted troth ;

And comfort us, and give abiding joy

To this your kingdom for an heir in whom

.Your excellence may live through every age."

Then Catharine said, " If God hath given me

    much,

Much must I love Him. But the man to whom

I give myself must be of noblest blood,

That all may worship him ; must be so great,

That he shall never think I made him king ;

For wealth must pass all others in the world ;

God's angels must desire to gaze on him,

As fairer than the sons of men ; while none

Can wrong him unforgiven, the most benign

Of princes. Till you find me such an one

I will remain mine own in maidenhood."

    " But thy desire lives not, nor ever lived."

" If him I find not, he shall yet find me,

For other will I none." And so she gave

Her careful labours to her people's weal,

Her love to Plato and the constant stars.

Now near her palace dwelt an aged man,

A hermit of Thebaid, who was wont

To live on roots, and sleep on the bare ground,

And daily chasten the rebellious flesh.

He thought on the bright Queen, and yearned to
    win

The treasure of her pure and ardent love

For the great Master whom he served ; so dreamed

That her heart's Lord should be the Son of GOD.

Then took he to her in a picture fair

The Maiden Mother and her Child Divine.

Who saved the world, and Catharine's soul was
    filled

So full of admiration for that Child

That study of the stars grew weariness,

And Plato's " Phaedrus " but a twice-told tale.

Dreaming, she met upon a mountain top

A white-robed throng of angels chapleted

With lilies, and she fell upon her face.

"Stand up, dear sister, and be welcome here,"

They said ; and led her to a goodlier throng

In purple clad, and crowned with roses red.

She fell before them, dazzled by their light,

And heard these words of greeting, tranced in joy :

"Stand up, dear sister Catharine. 'Tis thee

The King delights to honour." So they led

Her to a palace loftier than her own.

And there she saw the Maiden Mother throned.

To whom the angels said, "We bring to thee,

O Mother of the King of Blessedness,

Our sister, written in the book of life,

And pray thee take her for thy daughter." Then

Saint Mary led her to the Lord of all.

But He turned from her sadly, " Nay, for Me

She is not fair enough." So she awoke.

She, praised for peerless beauty heretofore,

Sought out the purport of this strange rebuff ;

She, who was spotless in the eyes of men,

17

Longed to be spotless before God, and prayed

For cleansing through His own unblemished Lamb,

Who bore the sin of all the world away ;

And in the laver of New Birth put off

Her old self, and put on the Christian name.

That night she saw the Holy Babe, and heard

Saint Mary say, " Lord, she hath been baptised,

And had me to her sponsor."   Then the Lord,

The Child born King, smiled on her, and she bent

In lowliest allegiance at His feet.

And lo ! it was a dream ; but on the hand

Lover ne'er pressed, she wore henceforth the pledge

Of that mysterious spousal to the Unseen :

Whithersoe'er He went, she followed Christ,

And as His bondmaid sat upon her throne.

Now Maximin the tyrant, hating Christ,

To Alexander's City came, and him

The devil filled with rage against God's saints,

Knowing his time was short, that soon the Cross

Would float victorious on the Empire's flag,

And heathendom be quelled by Constantine.

So the decree went forth : " Let holocausts

Be offered to the gods by high and low,

By all, from old men tottering to the tomb,

To sucklings whose unwitting hands must cast

A nameless grain on altars undiscerned."

Queen Catharine, fearing nothing for herself,

Much for her people, journeyed through the town,

Noisy with bleatings of devoted droves

Of sheep and oxen ; their poor lives outpoured,

The Christians' blood would crown the sacrifice.

She found the tyrant filling with his rites

The temple of Serapis ; entering in,

She faced him there, and claimed the right to plead

For her own Christian subjects, and to show

The glory of the faith of Christ to all.

Awed by her beauty and her queenliness,

He gave consent, and countless multitudes

Met to hear fifty sophists praise the gods,

And one meek woman speak for Jesus Christ.

But God was with her, drawn by fast and prayer

To lean upon His strength. " O Advocate

Of men, make me Thine advocate to-day,

And put Thy words upon my trembling lips,

That they may serve Thee, and may spare Thine
own."

So prayed she, and came out before the throng.

Knowing their highest wisdom, she showed
forth

God's higher wisdom : told them that the stars

Utter the One Creator's majesty ;

And gathered witness to a coming Christ

From sage and sibyl and from Hebrew seer.

Her mien was royal, passing fair her face,

Her voice was like the music of the spheres,

Her mellowed wisdom could not be gainsaid ; .

Consuming love for Him she called her Lord

Shone in her eye, and thrilled in every tone ;

Till all the sophists' arguments were hushed,

And fifty sages stood confessing Christ ;
And a great host believed on that great day.

Then Maximin waxed wroth exceedingly,
Baptising those believers in their blood ;
Bidding them hale the dauntless Christian maid
To torments keen.   Her tender limbs were drawn
Asunder on the rack, the dungeon dark
Closed on her, bruised and famished, left to die.
And there Faustina, wife of Maximin,
And Porphyry, his chief captain, sought her out,
Marvelling at her patience and her faith.
They in her lonely anguish found the saint
More glorious than when homage hemmed her
    round
On silken cushions in her palace set.
" I dreamed you offered me," the Empress said,
" A crown from Christ the Lord. Tell me of
    Him."
So Catharine spake of His redeeming love.

Wounded, she healed their wounded souls ; and
  bound,
She set them free ; in darkness, brought them light ;
And promised them the crown of martyrdom.
Both, three days later, suffered for the Faith.

Maximin, or the devil whom he served,
Still reeking with their blood, contrived for her
Unheard-of tortures : bound her to four wheels
Studded with spikes to rend her limb from limb.
But fire from heaven shattered them, and cast
Their fragments wide to scathe those sinful men,
And the sweet maid stood in the midst unharmed.

Thus the Lord proved His power to save His saint,
And baffle all devices of her foes.
Then, in His love, He took her quickly home.
For she had lived and testified, and braved
Bonds, agony, and death for His dear Name ;
And she was fair enough to enter now

The palace of the King with joy and mirth.

He let the tyrant hale her forth once more

Without the city, and the sword flashed high

And smote off her fair head. Then angels bright

Bore her pure body tenderly across

Red Sea and desert to its resting-place,

Hymning her triumph, praising God Most High,

Whose grace found consummation in this saint.

PHOINIKOPHOROS

(*Apoc. VII.* 9)

JOHN COLERIDGE PATTESON. BISHOP AND MARTYR
SLAIN AT NUKAPU, SEPTEMBER 20TH, A.D. 1871

" The white-robed army of Martyrs praise Thee "

A COFFER wrought of rare and fragrant wood
Grown 'neath the generous southern sun, but framed
By northern skill to guard a sacred thing,
Is opened to my reverent gaze : I see
The relics of a martyrdom, with thoughts
Of those who gathered round some altar tomb,
Where all the mortal of a faithful saint
Lay   shrined,   to   sing   their   fervent   hymns   to
    Christ,

When praising Him fetched death, and creeds were
    said
'Mid clamour of " The Christians to the lions ! "
Raised by a mob bloodthirsty as the beast
Who glared and gnashed upon them with his teeth,
And roared, outstretching his impatient fangs.

What tale is told by this long branch of palm,
Whose silver fronds are knotted with five knots ?

A tale of vengeance, where the Peaceful Sea
Catches the azures of a cloudless sky
Quivering and sparkling in its buoyant waves ;
Or thunders, churned to foam, upon a reef
The girdling fort of Melanesian shores.
The white man dreamed of Islands of the Blest
Long ages ere he stirred the still lagoon
Where floats the palm-crowned islet of the South,
And saw its coral forest and sea flowers
Of faery hue, or trod the glistening sands,

Or drank the balm of tropic breezes, fanned

By dense banane and waving cocoa-nut.

And when he came, he came in lust of gain,

Strong in his craft and cruelty, and took

Him labourers from the awed and 'wildered tribes.

So Nukapu had lost five dusky sons ;

And waited, wrathful, till a white man came

Alone, defenceless ; then the debt was paid,

Blind protest uttered, and his lifeless clay

Drifts out to sea, bearing on breathless breast

The knotted palm, to tell a speechless tale,

A tale of vengeance and a taken life.

A tale of love and of a given life ;

Claimed here, but given long ago to God,

A whole burnt-offering on His altar laid,

And sweet with incense in an English home,

Ere on this wise the higher summons came.

A faithful shepherd in the Church of Christ,

Whose heritage the utmost parts shall be,

Went forth to win the Australasian Isles

For Him, and as he said farewell he spake

In English ears the Hebrew prophet's song

Of all the sea's abundance turned to God,

Uttering the need that called him to go forth.

And one who heard him said to God, " Send
    me ! "

An eager boy, whom thirteen years had changed

Into an earnest man, when once again

That shepherd came, and quickened in his heart

The longing into purpose.   Offering then

What had been asked before, he cried, " Take me ! "

And thus forsaking all, he followed Christ

Even to Melanesia, where he toiled,

Christ's own bondservant, till the heathen folk

Tuned their soft speech to hymn the Crucified,

And praised Him yet more sweetly in their lives.

So sixteen years rolled on, and still he yearned

For those who had not heard and would not heed,

Seeking them out at peril of his life.

Ready not only to be bound for Christ,

But even to die for His dear Name.   He talked

Of Stephen to his true sons in the faith,

And landed on the island Nukapu.

They heard his voice no more.   They knew not
  when

The Son of Man received his spirit there.

But as that strange canoe came drifting up

They saw the smile of one at home with Christ,

Wounded with five wounds to the death, like
  Christ.

Now till the sea gives up its dead, he sleeps

Below the bright Pacific.   English eyes

Awestruck, within a stately house of prayer,

Beheld the relics of his martyrdom ;

No emblems of mortality, to tell

 `Of death and struggle, but the silvery branch

  That spoke to those of vengeance, and to these

Of that most valiant host through whom the Lord

Hath gotten Himself the victory, and shown

Salvation unto earth's remotest ends ;

Who follow Him, in robes of stainless white,

To life and triumph ever ; they must win

Till all the kingdoms of the world are His.

XII

THORA

MEMOIRS OF A NINETEENTH-CENTURY WOMAN

The over-curious public may wish to be informed at once that "Thora" is not an autobiography. The critics, ever ready to pounce upon the improbable in fiction, may be glad to know that the incidents of one real life are here interwoven with a few incidents taken from other real lives.

THORA

3ntroduction

I, MYRA, Randolph's wife, am legatee
To papers, signed and sealed by the dead hand
Of her who was my girlhood's dearest friend,
Sought out as lovers seek each other out,
The first of all not bound to me by blood
Or dearer bond of wedlock.   Why she gave
Her heart in such large measure unto me,
Who am not raised above the rest by aught,
I know not ; for in Thora powers met
That men had worshipped in a man, and owned
Even in a woman.   She would have me read
Her story, making others read it too
If it will guide or cheer a living soul.

Tears come not now as freely as they came

In girlhood, but my eyes o'erflowed yestreen

Reading it, when my dearest lord came in,

His day's work done, and drew me to his side,

And our lips met, as they meet every day,

Though we are wed for many a merry year ;

And since the hour my maiden love went out

To meet the sweetest lover in the world,

Tall lads and girls have filled our home, and
Time

Has furrowed cheek and slackened youthful gait.

Still we are lovers, lovers we shall be

When eld has crowned our brows with arctic
snow.

Devotion deepens, nestling in the arms

Of the protecting love which shields my head :

I could conceive that failing me as soon

As I repenting that I gave away

Myself, and sat to learn at Love's own feet

One summer, nearly forty years ago.

But what am I, that life to me has brought

Its best in such abundance, when for her

Who had turned its sunshine into richer fruit,

Such cloudy days made up a dreary year?

I ask it, as I ask those glowing woods

Why death must be their portion, when they
  stand

Most glorious in their gold and crimson robes.

Thus Thora's noble character shone out

Most noble, when she bowed her head in
  death.

Read me the riddle through an emblem true.

"As a tree's days my people's days shall be,"

Said a great prophet. Even trees take heart

To pluck best radiance from the ageless sun

Ere they without misgiving lay aside

Their robes, and face the winter blast unclothed,

Knowing they die not all, and Spring must come,

When buds of hope will bloom and promise fruit.

So man, who has For Ever, dares to wait.

Part I

PARENTAGE

AUSTEN, the earl's tall son, loved Adela ;

But she could never give him love for love.

They praised him, he was comely, well-endowed,

Blameless withal, and born of high degree ;

And none could gainsay aught of all their praise.

She smiled on him, and not on him alone.

Some reckoned her the sweetest girl they knew :

While others, carping, saw in sunny speech

That asked for praise and sunny speech again,

A soul by shallow liking whilome stirred,

Where deep, devoted love could never shrine.

Yet might a kindred, higher soul have changed

Light girl to tender woman, had one made

Her heart beat quick for him.   Here Austen
  failed.

" I find no fault.   Nay, he is good, too good ;

But I could never love him."   " Were he old,

Lowborn, or evil, I would urge thee not,"

Her mother said, " but I would die content

Could my girls' faces win me five such sons.

Maids that are too nice often die unwed."

" Better keep hand than give without the heart,"

Cried Adela.   " Schoolgirl romance, have done !

When thou hast followed three fair brides to
  church,

And none hath led thee to its altar veiled,

Thou wilt be wise too late.   Thy cold esteem

Is the dull sheath where folded petals sleep

In darkness now, that wedlock will call forth

To perfect bloom of sober, wifely love.

But girlhood's passing fancy kindled swift

To passionate love is like untimely bloom

Preventing its own foliage, when raw winds

Beat their chill wings on the bare boughs of
    March ;

Bloom that will lie unheeded, trodden, soiled,

When patient blossom wakes 'neath kinder skies.

Leave then the figment of the fairy tale

For facts, as childhood's whims are left for life."

She faltered, till the devil came and said,

" Austen is rich.   Let pomp and ease be yours."

Then Austen asked again, and had to wife

Her who could take Love's sacred name in vain.

And never blither bridegroom fitted ring

On whiter finger.   He indeed was rich

As men count riches ; in high places set,

Though not in highest ; he had wooed and won

Knowledge, which brought him fame, and fame
    brought friends.

Yet he was poor in greater things than these.

His mother gave him life which cost her death ;

His father died ere he could shrink from death ;

His brothers went their ways that were not his.

He, yearning vainly to be all to one

Who should be all to him, gave Adela

Frankest affection, trusting her reserve

Mantled a heart as ardent as his own.

Had she not sworn to love him utterly?

Men marked them as a happy man and wife.

"Good fortune follows some from dawn to eve :

Austen, who had so much, has won yet more.

How well her neck becomes his heirloom pearls !

How well she fills his hall with willing guests !

How smoothly runs his life !   How fine the brood—

Two sons, three daughters—who adorn their
    home ! "

And yet soul-hunger wans his placid face.

That which he had in form and hue was like

The bread he craved for, but it proved a stone ;

Whose unappeasing hardness thus he learned.

One day, his arm about his new-made wife,

He told her how he wept himself to sleep

In lonely crib, seeing another child

Laid by a mother's kind, strong hands to rest,

His prayer murmured at her knee, his lids

Sealed for their careless sleep by her fond kiss.

Then Adela said, "'Tis strange to recollect

What paltry joys and woes made up our life

Ere we had put our childish things away."

Bankrupt of love, she'd live without a tear ;

While he would long to die.   Her bond to pay

Him love was paper promise to the end ;

And all his aims and hopes were strange to her.

He planned, 'mid murmuring pines and new-mown
    hay,

For joy in sunshine shared by singing birds,

A haven from turmoil of their London life.

She planned to fill that new abode with guests,

For her perpetual quest of life's delight.

" Have I not earned the peace of solitude ? "

" Nay, we shall find it passing dull alone."

He pled for leisure to bring forth a book

Germinate in the darkness of his brain,

A darling sprout of fancy, ripe to shoot.

She doubted not 'twas clever, 'twould be praised ;

But she, who never read, believed the world

Was over-full of books, and time was scant

For literary idlesse : duties throng,

When sons must be advanced and daughters wed,

And clamouring society satisfied.

The world called her " good mother " not amiss,

True daughter of her mother, whose own girls

Edna and Dona like herself would grow,

Though wilful Thora, youngest of the flock,

Might disappoint.   Her tale is written here

For who would learn the story of her soul.

Part II

CHILDHOOD

THORA was five when Austen found the child,
With trace of recent tempest on her face,
Hovering near his study.   He, her friend
And champion ever, bore her off to bliss
Beside him, hearing that the time had come
When she, who had already learned to love
The language of the printed page, must know
Language of ivory keys she could but hate.
Her uttered hate had been rebuked : " Come back
At noon in better mind and take your task."
But noon long past, she sat at Austen's feet ;
And as warm airs and ruddy hues return
To the discouraged scene when clouds drift off,

Lightened of rain, and leave the sun unveiled,

Her smiles brake forth. " Oh, mother, could you
   guess

The moth wore feathers like a downy dove ?

Through these great eyes has father shown them
   me."

But Adela entering, greeted thus, replied,

" What dost thou here, wasting thy precious time,

Thy father's, and thy teacher's ? Hence, forthwith ! "

Then to her husband, " Thora will not learn.

' Apt pupil ' sayest thou ?   Nay, I spoke of things

Worth learning for a girl whose dower of face

Is poorer than her sisters'.   Little boots

Knowing a beetle's legs are six or eight ;

While girls who play and sing can always charm."

Then Austen, " Said Petruchio, Kate for me

Rather than smooth Bianca, and said well."

Part III

GIRLHOOD

THORA at fifteen yielded beauty's praise
To Dona, her fair mother's fairest child,
And Edna, who with white, well-moulded arm,
Swept harp-strings into winning melody :
Not humbly wooing music as an art,
But leading captive an accomplishment
That promised finer captives in its train.
Serene in self-contentment with their caste,
Their faultless features, and their faultless guise,
Were both.   They reckoned as their breath of life
The dainty adulation which blows round
Womanhood fair and young and rich ; claimed this,
Even as they claimed soft couch and sheeny robes

And hothouse blossom for their jewelled throats.

Life gave them all that life can give to such.

And they were gracious to their friends, and kind

To needy ones who crossed their flowery path,

Nor checked their progress.   Dona's sweetest smile

Was given to twenty friends, who each believed

Herself its only owner.   And they said,

"So gentle and affectionate a maid

Will be a loving wife ere long.   'Tis well

Strong-minded Thora weds her books so soon,

For she is cold and strange and hath scant charm."

They said so, looking on her ruffled hair,

Shy bearing, fixed blue eyes, and mobile mouth's

Thwarted expression.   She already longed

To make the world anew, and find a scope

For untried powers fellow-men might need.

"I can do something: much is there to do."

And those who saw her kindling at such words

Called her lit face the fairest of the three.

While her few friends were grappled to her soul

Once and for ever. Austen's long-starved heart
Proved hers the warmest he had ever sought.
She loved to browse among his books and brood
On questionings hard of action and of thought.
The grave professor, with his thin grey locks
And scholar's stoop, who talked to her an hour
Of Sophocles and Plato (while the rest
Wondered what two who could not tune their
  tongues
To topics of the moment found to say),
Deemed her the best of comrades in discourse,
Joining man's earnestness to woman's wit.
Then his last essay on the true import
Of great Athene Glaukopis he gave
And she took, blushing deep with eager joy,
Panting for knowledge : till another guest
Laid hold of her and catechised her thus :—
" Say, are you fond of music ? "   " Dona plays,
Not I."   " Then do you sing ? "   " I must begin
Next year, I fear."   " Then is your pencil skilled ? "

"Nay, Edna is the artist of our group."

"So you have no pursuits. We cannot all

Be clever." Thora meekly held her peace,

Weighed and found wanting in the worldling's
scale,

And heard a verdict harder still to bear.

"Thora is clever, not like other girls ;

She should have been a boy." Then Thora took

Indignant " Wherefore ? " to her happiest haunt,

Where Austen, having given to the state

His morning hours, gleaned from the social eve

Time for the self-set task that is not toil.

His gathered lore of many climes and books

Were shaping forth a volume on the use

Worldwide of Lions as heraldic signs.

There Thora, when her tale of bricks was told,

Piano, sketching, dancing, singing, French,

Stole to her father's window-seat and mused ;

Lived in the age of chivalry, and read

Of fearless, stainless Bayard, as the sun

Shed last rays on the knighted window pane ;

Or gazed upon one helmèd marble head—

Pallas Athene—with her soul aflame

To learn the language of those godlike Greeks,

Key to the storehouse of the world's best thought.

" What saith Athene to my pensive maid ? "

Asked Austen.   And she burst forth, all aglow,

" Why, if the Greeks, the wisest of mankind,

Called Wisdom goddess and not god, do men

Refuse the tree of knowledge unto us,

And grudge to women all the joys of fame ? "

" Not so ; for wise Hypatia's pupils found

Her Pallas in the flesh ; and Rome's best king

Was tutored by Egeria the nymph ;

Learned Apollos sat at Prisca's feet ;

And, in Bologna, students flocked to hear

Professors erudite as they were fair.

Strong women have been gladly owned as strong,

Since Deborah and Hatasu bore rule ;

And social queens were queens of culture too

When great Elizabeth made England great."

"Why was I born out of that happier past?

I have a mind that craves for solid food,

That I may gird me unto worthy work.

But blind convention gives me husks for grain,

And bids me sit aloft and idly sing,

Mocking the toilers amid unknown ills,

That surge and seethe below and will o'erwhelm

Toilers and singers unredressed at last.

They shut us out from the wide world of thought,

Then blame our trivial hopes and petty aims.

Oh, could I win for women lore that men

Take not when offered! Had I Vernon's chance,

Think you I'd call it sacrifice to make

Some leisure from the oar for 'those old books'

That are withheld where craved? Oh, to amend

The scheme of gentle life that rules to-day!"

"Self must be mended ere we mend the world,"

Said Austen. "Thora, you shall seek and find.

My book accomplished, I will teach you Greek,

19

Filling your basket with good grain to grow

Unto good harvest if you sow aright.

For flattery as woman, you shall earn

Honour as human being, using well

The powers God has given to my child."

    Thora received her Greek books at the time

Trees and young maids adorn themselves for play.

Then pretty Dona donned a dainty robe

Snowy as is the one soft cloud that hangs

Alone in June's deep blue, and knelt to kiss

The sovereign's hand, returned elate, and cried,

" Oh, Thora, long you not to go to court ? "

Blunt was the answer, " I would rather go

To college." " What ? To waste your brightest
    days

Painfully gaining dusty lore, which gained

Is vain, unless you mean to die ' old maid ' ? "

" I mean to prove us born for higher things

Than pleasing all men for a little space,

To be the slave of one's caprice for aye."

" Well, let me not provoke the world to say

My learning left me lonely," Edna scoffed.

And Thora, blazing, mentioned her who wrote

" Aurora Leigh," and her who mapped the heavens.

Had ever two such women died unwed ?

Then went off proudly gleeful for her first

And last Greek lesson, at her father's side.

The birds were singing in the dawn next day,

When Austen, racked with anguish, said farewell

To kith and kin, to all he had achieved,

To infant schemes and projects yet unborn,

Seized suddenly of Death.   His children slipped

Asunder like unthreaded beads henceforth.

And his unloving wife harsh mother proved

To Thora, crude, imperfect creature, loth

To bow to her perfection ; problem strange,

She cared not to unriddle.   One short word,

Like thistledown, revealed the north-east wind.

The sisters sat around a lamp one eve,

Which Thora's quick impatient movement felled :

Her sleeve rushed up in flame, but she was saved;

Thanked God first, and sought out her mother next.

And Adela said only, "Heedless girl!

Dear Edna has been shaken with alarm."

Her firstborn's paltry fear weighed with her more

Than the dire peril of her youngest child.

Poor Thora, youth's unbridled hopes immerged

In measureless despair, laid down her head

On the closed Greek books in her father's room;

Thought of her visioned volume, dedicate

To him who led her from the common plain

Toward breezy uplands of a larger life;

And sobbed, "Oh, father, not one word of love

From thee, who hadst my heart before all else,

Shall I hear ever on this side the grave!

Mother and sisters love me, I must fear,

As little as they understand my soul.

So I have only God, vast, distant Love,

Needing a mirror in some human heart

Ere we can feed our hungry hearts withal."

Part IV

WOMANHOOD

THORA at twenty-five was one of three
Peopling the nest that once had compassed seven.
The gallant Walter perished, face to foe,
Widening the wide bounds of Britannia's rule ;
Adela, two years widowed, mourned him sore.
Vernon had cure of distant village souls,
Living in credit days with no strong hue.
While of his sisters one was wedded wife.
Hugh, with fat rentroll, sought a gentle thing
To soothe his feebleness of gathering eld ;
A pretty thing to adorn with all his gold ;
A thing to fondle by his calm fireside ;
And found all these in Dona, and for these

Gives name and lands and rich attire, and adds,

Since woman must some helpless fondling have,

A milk-white greyhound in a silver chain.

Rachel preventing Leah chafed the soul

Of Edna, and she fastened on a youth

Who paid a casual homage at their house,

And let them say that she had been betrothed.

Thora was no more the unlessoned girl,

Openly scorning common social aims ;

Talking of Pallas with an aged don

Beneath the pitying eyes of kith and kin ;

Beating her foolish head 'gainst the blind bricks

Of dull convention that closed in her life.

She had reached after many things withheld,

Groping towards ideals far too vast

For her embrace, and yearning to outsoar

On wings of knowledge the confining wall.

Now, slowly learning that to stretch out wings

Were swift uncertain gain, so we must climb,

Being unwinged, and footsore win our way,

By brake and cliff and bog to baffling peak,

If none can show us where the paths are cut ;

She climbed alone, in patient diligence,

Climbed with no boisterous blazon of her toil ;

But as we curtain o'er the imaged face

Of one we love, that those share not our sight

Who share not our affection, Thora hid

Her soul, and conned the art of trivial chat ;

Crude scorn of marriage passed her lips no more ;

She shrank from common banter on that theme,

As she had shrunk from those who laid rude hands

Upon the Holy Table of the Lord.

She shunned unlikeness to her kind in aught ;

Proving more like them than she guessed one day.

    Roused on her birthday morn by countless birds

Twittering " Good-morrow " to the earliest sun

Of June, from slumbers healthful as their own,

She from her open window watched the trees,

Swaying untarnished branches each on each,

And drew in draughts of fragrant morning air,

Till her whole being pulsed with joyous life.

The lawns, that drank their fill of grateful dew

Through the short night, sparkled with countless
　　gems

As the sun sifted out his threefold light

To countless dewdrops, and the hidden lark

Poured forth a torrent of wild melody ;

No wordless song, but echoing one name,

The sweetest human lips can utter—Love.

" He loves me." Dare she dream so bright a
　　dream,

Throbbing from head to foot with ecstasy,

First rapture of a holy, happy love,

Too vague to utter even in prayer to God ?

Yes, there was one for whom she lifted up

The veil that wrapped her from the common gaze :

Gerald, her father's kinsman, kin in mind

As in his noble lineage, lately come

From travel earned by gleaming college palms.

She felt his eyes upon her in a throng,

And grew more beautiful beneath his gaze.

She found him waiting patient at her side

For chance of talk beyond the weary round

Of " He did," " She said," " They were surely here."

Gossip of mere acquaintance was not theirs,

Nor trifling flattery 'twixt man and maid,

But earnest converse of two human hearts,

Wherein God placed eternity, as saith

Koheleth : * how to find out conquering truth,

So that our life be more than meat, our joy

Greater than ease.   She told him that she yearned

To sit at Plato's feet ; and then he brought

His well-worn Plato, and to " Phædo " turned;

Asking her to accept a bust of him

Who into the profound of human thought

Had dropt so deep a plummet ; bringing too

A porcelain toy for Edna, and vague words

Of pleasant evenings spent with Adela ;

Worshipping still the virgin pride which made

* Ecclesiastes iii. 11.   Revised Version.

More clamorous love presumption.   Thora found

Converse with him the richest she had known

Since Austen's cultured gentleness had passed

Out of her life, and reckoned up the days

To promised sojourn 'neath his mother's roof.

All else was in a luminous haze that hid

The fair Manoa whither she drew nigh,

That golden city some have found on earth,

That some have scorned, and many sought in vain.

Till snatch of handmaids' gossip reached her ears ,

Touching herself and Edna.   " Goods that lie

Beseeching purchase in the sun and rain

Are oft unsold, while others are fetched forth

For pleading buyers from the inner store.

Miss Thora will be first to wed, and rule

The castle that she visits ; if my lord

Has his way she will be my lady soon."

   As Thora from her window leaned that morn

Light fell on much that had been dark before.

She thought of the loved father she had lost,

Of the cold-hearted mother whom in vain

She tried to love, and how against her will

Edna had made her strange. Then dreamed of life

Lighted by hourly lavished love of one

To whom she was supreme in all the world.

Womanhood woke within her as she knew

'Tis sweet to take and sweeter still to give

Bounty untold of all the love we hold

Dammed up for lack of outlet till it seethes.

" Oh, let me lose myself, to find myself

In one far greater ! Let me spend my days

To halve his loads and double all his joys ;

Till two lives welded each to each shall shape

Both incomplete unto a perfect whole ;

Each raising each by mutual love and trust,

Till both become what each deems each to be.

Till the lone stream that forced its troubled way

Through tangled channel and o'er boulders rude

Glide into the still lake, and happy flow

Embraced by wider waters than its own."

Souls grow by such new thoughts and such sweet
    dreams,
Though the awaking be to dreary day.

    News! He whom Edna claimed as all her own
Wedded another. Edna gave one cry,
" I have lived long enough," and hid herself
I' the turret chamber. Two hours later came
A scared handmaiden, who had plucked her back
From the bare ledge whence she would hurl herself.
So saved her for this world a further space
Who had untimely dashed against the doors
That shut out the encompassing unknown,
In midst of which we live our little lives.
Dim doors, whose hinges ever hither turn
To let the dying crowd pass out thereat ;
But never turned they thither that the dead
Come back, save once when One drew nigh to
    them,
The only one of all the sons of men
Who died because He willed to die, since Death

Could never claim Him who was sinless else.

Then those dread portals fell before His might,

And souls that fluttered on the threshold passed

Out into sunlight ; and He filled that realm,

Where spirits dwell unseen, with such a ray

From His pure presence that He left it bright

To all for whom He conquered Death henceforth.

    Edna, snatched sudden back to life, returned

Slowly to reason ; but that maddened deed

Could never more for Thora be undone.

See her now proved and humbled in the vale

Of her decision, when she paced the lawn

Pondering this letter : " Thora dear, we count

Upon your promised visit.   Come alone,

If Edna's recent illness leaves her weak."

Things seen and heard and guessed whirled through

    her brain :

Adela's mother passed from sight of all

In Thora's childhood ; her abode was veiled

In vaguest phrase ; nor was she greatly wept

When she deceased, because her body lived

Too long, a prison-house of aspect drear

That mocked the purpose of the informing soul.

The taint of madness oftener passes on

To children's children than to children ; so

Dona in dawning womanhood had gone

To strange seclusion ; 'twas explained at last ;

Together with that word concerning her,

Departing bride, " She'll be a childless wife,

'Tis well." She thought of Edna's wild weird
　　ways,

And of the gusts of passion sweeping o'er

Her own soul, only to be calmed by prayer.

Now, should she let that seedling plant of love

Grow till he asked and had, and she should bring

Upon the honoured house of him she loved

A curse for dowry? Should he ask in vain,

And deem her heartless since she could not say,

" I love not," nor disclose that secret dread?

The lips of all who knew were sealed with gold.

" Oh, Gerald ! do I love you now so well

That you must never utterly love me ;

And must we never meet again, lest love

Grow up between us irreversibly ? "

She stood as on a Highland ridge that parts

A smiling pasture grazed by happy flocks

And set in murmuring woods and waving corn,

Yellowing 'neath tranquil sunshine, from a moor

Bare save for horrid rocks, where gathering clouds

Empty them pitiless on the barren ground.

Free at that moment, never free again,

To go down either slope ; her choice of life

Before her.   Then she poured out all her soul

In throbbing prayer.   " O God, our wills are weak,

Our flesh is weaker than our wills.   Give grace,

And I will dash the untasted cup of joy

From my dry lips, if 'tis not filled by Thee."

But Gerald's mother grieved to miss her guest

And grudged that she must travel forth to please

Adela's whim for selfish Edna's health.

So Thora made her ready to depart

For two years' exile, glad to crowd her days

And leave no space for thought. They brought
    to her

A letter from her girlhood's dearest friend

As she put out to sea, wherein she read

Myra in three short months will be a bride.

" She will go down the sunny side of life,

While roses pouring o'er the garden wall

Bend fragrant clusters toward her as she moves

Amid men's benedictions, in the light

Of one great love that is her own for aye.

While I go down the shady side alone

For evermore, and withered leaflets torn

From trees autumnal ere the summer ends

Dance in my path before the stripping wind.

Oh, let my love for her be strong enough

To cast out envy ! I rejoice for her,

Hiding my heart from the harsh world that sees

In me a scorner of the holiest joys

That fall to woman ; while the years stretch out
To the blank future, and my surging thoughts
Die childless, as I die, no kindred mind
Quickening them into purpose. Once I cried
In girlhood, I had only God, and longed
To know His love through human love ; but now
In unrecorded sacrifice to right,
I cast away the dearest thing on earth,
Suffering loss of love for love's sweet sake.
Then God shall be my All, so He but use
My life in work for Him and His, and fill
My craving heart with His unmeasured love."

Part V

FAME

THORA was thirty-five when she attained
Her childhood's dream of fame for man's work
  done
And man's reward achieved.   There are who hold
No woman should be sung, whose golden dawn
Has passed into the greyer sky of noon.
Rightly, if woman can fulfil her end
Ministering to the lower self of man.
If houri for his pastime, let us sing
Peach bloom and sparkling eyes of earliest youth.
If squaw to ease him of life's lowlier tasks
And roast what he hath taken in the chase,
Sing of her youthful strength and scorn her age.

But if the man and woman are alike,

Undying spirits lodged in fleshly tents

That each lift other to a higher life,

Then added years are added gain for both.

So we who tell the story of a soul

Writing its record on an aging face,

Note peach bloom withering in the taint of that

Which maketh for unrighteousness, or else

Transfigured into beauty ne'er attained

In half-awakened, untaught girlhood's days ;

Drawn upward by no formless Power for good,

But by the Being who alone is good,

And made His creatures unto holiness.

Thora grew homeless when she might have won

A home for all her days, and wept farewell

To Austen's study, sweet with memories,

Gathering her heritage from out its shelves.

Then wandered with her kindred, wandering still,

Wherefore they knew not, when to port they
steered ;   .

Roaming through many lands with open eyes,

Learning new races and new languages,

Waiting for news that, Gerald's fancy spent,

He made another happiest wife on earth.

So five years passed, until she stood again

A stranger in the greatest City's throng,

Bidden by a friend she made beyond the seas

To a strange house to meet an unknown
    group.

There, 'mid the clash of music, she o'erheard

The hostess welcoming her guest of guests,

" Give me the joy of bringing face to face

Two clever friends.   I trust she still is here."

And then came tones that thrilled her through and
    through,

" My fair kinswoman.   Has she then returned ? "

Louder the music clashed, and through it rang

A voice, " Stay but a moment till it cease.

You yet may be the happiest woman born.

Let not a baseless scruple wreck his life."

That voice prevailed not. From the house she
  passed,
A lonely woman, lost in London's sea.
And the world wondered Gerald did not wed.

Then five more uneventful years rolled on,
And she grew lonelier. Vernon brought a bride
To an ivied parsonage ; and Adela
Ended her days beside his hearth, well-pleased
That Edna had attained her goal at last,
By wedding one younger in years than she,
 Though older than she named herself to him,
Donning her girlish bridal bravery,
In days when Thora likewise reached her goal.
  She sits among her books, with Plato's bust
For sole adornment of her busy room.
Her letters come, kindling her face with joy.
" My book, the darling offspring of my thought,
Sells fast, and they commend it ; better still,
It promises to light in this world's gloom

A little candle that the wayfarer

May bless me for, who else had lost his road.

Again—and yet again—they ask for more

From the bold pen that wrote on " Woman's Call,"

And claimed for her what Time shall yet concede.

I have done more than I had hoped to do.

So has God turned my loss to higher gain

For other women, and I live to prove

There may be room and honour in the world

For the unwed whose lives are fruitful found."

Fair Myra entered as she thus rejoiced,

Bringing her smallest son and fragrant flowers ;

" For you must know that praise of Myra's friend

In all men's lips is Myra's happiness.

We, who could never think your clever thoughts,

Are proud a woman thinks them, envying you."

So Myra ever like the sunshine fell

On Thora's path, reflecting from her face

Tranquil felicity of homely life,

Lived out by those the world will never name ;

Yet envying the famous, not with dumb

And sullen envy, nearly all blind grief

You should have that I taste not nor deserve ;

But generous envy, nearly all pure joy

Outspoken, that your cup is brimming o'er,

Be mine or full or empty, since I love

You, with the love that longs to give, and longs

That others likewise love and give to you.

   Now, while they talked on the exhaustless theme

Of Thora's book, the child had fallen asleep ;

Whom Thora gathered in her arms at length,

And bore, scarce wakened, to his little car.

Then, when its wheels went echoing down the
    street,

A strangely sudden cloud o'ercast her sky,

Cloudless an hour ago.   So I have seen

A lake, as gentian blue, as mirror calm,

Turn in a moment, when the envious grey

Rolls from the hilltop, into leaden-hued

And restless ripples. Thora bowed her head,

Weeping the unheeded tears of lonely grief.

Sudden uplifting often searches out,

Like sudden sorrow, tracts left unexplored

In common days.   She read herself anew

In a new light from those blue eyes, half-veiled

By sleepy lids, that flushed cheek on her face,

And those warm arms laid trustful on her neck.

"Envy me!   She, to whom that nursling cried,

'Mother,' and leapt from out my arms to hers!"

Then waters bubbled from the deepest fount

Of her emotion, whence the stone was rolled.

"O Myra, radiant in your growing joy,

I deemed you happy when your love was won ;

Yet happier when I met you, new-made wife,

Amid the chestnuts at Fiesole ;

Yet happier when the tardy spring had come

To mild San Remo first, where oft we saw

That pretty babe whose pale young mother died,

At sight of whom I marked your beaming face

Lit with the secret of a coming joy,

Beautiful, beautifying motherhood ;

Your being ripened by strong love called forth,

Renewing youth once more as each new babe

Cried to you in its gladly succoured need.

While faster than its wont the fleeting bloom

Of maidenhood we women prize did fleet

From lips that never knew a lover's kiss,

And cheeks that dimpled fingers ne'er caressed.

Mine is an unwept loss, and yet methinks

One greater than the loss they bade me weep,

Telling last week of four Septembers past.

The first when Gwennyth showed upon her hand

Love's glittering pledge, and playful pity claimed

For all her sisters, ' Whosoe'er they wed

The noblest of mankind is mine alone.'

The second when a plainer pledge turned troth

To wedlock, and farewell to girlhood came.

The third when two linked lives made common

   joy

Over the new life given to their charge.

The fourth when death did part till death is past

Those whom God joined, and severed for a space

To knit again the ravelled web of love

When all is made anew for all whose death

Is but the portal to a larger life,

A deeper love and an abiding joy.

Weep for her ! She has been a happy wife,

She is a blessed mother still, and knows

Our Lord's own symbol of intensest bliss.

'Poor Gwennyth!' do they idly say? I cry,

'Rich Gwennyth!' If I must bemoan a lot

Let it be Brenda's ; note her empty past

And dreary future, blank of human love.

A rich man's child reared to be rich man's wife,

Untaught in aught that teaches, but equipped

With flimsiest accomplishments for show ;

Drifting from flower to flower in balmy spring

Of thoughtless youth, until her plumes were
   dimmed

By fresher butterflies that shared her lawn.

Her father died ; her brother took a wife ;

She left the spacious home with all its mirth,

Lived in a little house a narrow life,

Narrowing each season, tended by a maid,

Two songsters and a cat for company ;

The dew of youth and morning all exhaled,

The chillier dews of evening not yet fallen ;

Not poor enough to find in daily bread

A summons to attempt, nor rich enough

To roam the world in quest of new delights ;

Ignorance and conventions of her caste

Cutting her off from joy in enterprise

Of deed worth doing ; waking morn by morn

To aimless days ; and longing all in vain

That she were needed by one human soul.

" When a man, strong in self-control, lives out

A single life, owning no woman's love

Save his inheritance of mother's kiss

And sister's calm affection, when his lips

Have never met the warmth of other lips,

Chosen from all the world and wooed and won,

His love goes out on some great work for man,

For God's sake and his brother's ; wedding this,

As did the prophet priest of Anathoth,

Or Plato, or Saint Francis long ago,

Or Melanesia's martyred bishop now ;

Then all men honour his devoted zeal.

And even if he marries humbler toil,

And his dull days and strangled cravings prove

It is not good that man should be alone ;

None judge his choice of life nor hold him cheap.

But all will point the ready gibe at her

Who dies ' old maid,' departing undesired,

Like Joram, who outwore his people's love.

Gone is the simple happiness of old,

When each young maiden was besought of some,

And each might hope to make a home and know

A husband's care and children at her knee.

But now the lads go even beyond the bounds

Of our world-girdling empire, from the isle

Too narrow for adventure, work, and gain,

Laying foundations in some virgin soil

For future homes when unborn maids are wived.

Meanwhile the maids these wanderers might have
won

Shrivel at home, like plants in cellars reared,

Wherein the sun and air can take no joy,

Their love unclaimed, their lives devoid of aim.

And modern gaslights shame the tender glow

Of mediæval lamps that lit the brows

Of maids with worshipped radiance all their days.

Ah ! those old times when God's world first shook
off

License of Paganism, as a man

Shakes off a glittering snake whose guileful tongue

Plays in his bosom with intent to wound,

Exalted mere virginity as first

Foothold to sainthood, and with mystic zeal

Wove round the Virgin who bore God fine wefts

Of legend, fair and fleeting as the veil

Of summer gossamer, wherein they saw

(Fond fancy) fragments of Our Lady's shroud,

Dropped earthward when she was upborne to
    Heaven,

The crowning day of Christian womanhood.*

But we have wakened ; these dim dreams are fled,

And holy wedlock claims its rightful place

As symbol of the mysteries of God ;

With awful obligation, Give away

All that thou hast, and yield thee body and soul,

Heartwhole surrender thou hast vowed to one,

Fearless, undoubting in thine utter trust ;

Then take the untold wealth of unguessed love

That can enrich thy life beyond all dreams.

Christ and His Church are shadowed by such
    bonds.

But loveless life is like a torrent bed,

Barren and dusty, till the prisoned spring,

---

* In accordance with this mediæval fancy, " Gossamer
to be a corruption of " God's mother."

Yearning to lose itself in ocean's deeps,

Gush sunlit from the heights, and warble down

The dry defile, making it laugh with bloom,

Primrose and grass and fern and scented thyme.

Such might have been my life, and none had
    blamed

Save God's own voice of conscience in my soul.

Now the harsh world thinks I would dare contemn

Unoffered blessings, as I pitied once

The pretty face, light heart, unfurnished head,

And low ambition of the average girl.

Are there not tears that soothe and tears that
    sting ?

And mine are tears that sting.   O mocking Fame,

Your dazzling phantom lured me once ; but now

'Twixt me and you a golden childish head

Tells me that Shakespeare's fame were not enough

To fill a woman's heart, or match the joy

A toiling peasant knows whose ruddy babe

Coos for caresses when her work is done.

And yet there is who casts her babe aside
To hirelings, wearying of her last new toy,
So that it grow up one more useless man,
One more ungrateful mother's lost reward,
While all the unused passion of my soul
Lies strangling with abiding sense of loss.
God, feed the hungry hearts that Thou hast made,
Or we go starved and feeble all our days !
Christ, comfort me, who unto one meek Maid
Once gav'st the purest joy of motherhood
That ever woman knew on Thy sad earth ! "

" Yes, you have laboured unto weariness,
Lay pen aside and leave the unquiet town,
Then health and spirits will again be yours."
So Thora took this counsel, and retired
Whither her father ofttimes loved to go,
And bade them lay him for his last long sleep,
In God's calm country, whose slow rivers slip
By undulating mead and dusky copse.

'Twas evening on the day the faithful keep
Sacred to Christ, risen from death thereon.
And Thora worshipped in the little church,
Beneath the semblance of her ancestor,
Who poured out gold and blood to serve the King
When rude rebellion shook the fevered state.
The murmured music of the evening hymn
Floats o'er the churchyard from the opened panes,
And as they leave, glad faces tell of hearts
Lifted by prayer from earth. The peaceful scene
Swims in the radiance of the westering sun,
Till even common things are glorified.
Then Thora threads, waistdeep in yellowing corn,
The little path across the hill, and sees
A village lad and maiden, arms entwined,
Tasting the Paradise young lovers know,
As all the woe that grew from Adam's sin
Were a bad dream they had awakened from.
While lonely Thora, on whose love none leaned
Since Austen died, was passing to her grave,

Where love and hate alike are quenched in gloom,

With none to ask the love she had to give.

Now came she to a cot beset with clumps

Of cheerful, homely flowers; creepers flung

Bright petals o'er the casement; in the porch

Rested a blind and aged village dame,

Her toilworn hands folded upon her knee,

In this still sabbath evening of her life.

And on the doorstep sat three little maids,

Singing a hymn for childish joy of song.

"Yes, Jesus loves me," was its glad refrain.

The love of God had been in Thora's ears

Since first she learned the simple text with glee,

And bore the sermon on it, deadly dull,

Envying the flies that o'er the tablets buzzed

And danced while she sat still in the tall pew.

And in her chamber hung a picture, limned

By an early master, of the Cross whereon

God stooped to save, Man lifted up mankind.

Knowing that this great Love had been, she made

Her prayer at morn and eve ; but the child's song

Flashed on her as a heaven-sent bird might shoot

Into a fog-encompassed atmosphere,

Which only ravens haunted heretofore,

Its plumage painted by the lavish sun

Of far-off tropics.   To her heart of hearts

The message reached, and bore her on the tide

Of high emotion, echoing the words

Of Shulammith, the humble village maid,

Besought by the great King of Israel

(Bright in the undimmed splendour of his youth,

Whom all men did beseech), for stately neck

As white as David's tower, soft doves' eyes,

And feet that shone in Mahanaim's dance,

The lowly object of a lofty love,

Fronting that homage, humbly proud to say,

" Lo, my Beloved is mine and I am his."

Thora's heart sang : " I go not undesired,

The infinite Redeemer asks my love,

And deigns to need the meanest He has made."

Part VI

WHEREUNTO?

THORA is forty-five, when once again

We meet the sisters of our lengthening tale,

Maid, wife, and widow.   Edna cries as wife,

Vainly desiring she were still a maid,

" May I be widow or he widower soon ! "

Now she had married for the matron's name,

Ralph to repair his fortunes with her gold.

Each object was attained ; then, why lament

That what they sought not was not likewise

    found ?

But if 'tis woman's highest lot to find

Nobler ideal in a noble real,

Moulding the real by her faith and hope

And love to that ideal day by day,

Till latent evil dies and latent good

Springs forth triumphant ; 'tis her deepest woe

To sell herself for sustenance or pomp,

Vowing the utter fealty of wife

To one scarce known, or honoured not at all.

If holy wedlock is in Heaven made ;

This wedlock's fetters must be forged in hell.

    Near Hugh's tall mausoleum Dona's days

Flowed on uncounted in their placid ebb.

She trod life's highway, worn by million feet,

With dainty step and delicate garb, and men

Praised that she walked the lower path so well.

While Thora flung aside the gauds of ease,

Breasted the lonely mountain, stumbling oft

And halting on the rugged, pathless side,

Yet ever climbing toward the wider view.

And half the world exclaimed, " Why climb at
    all ? "

And half, " Why climbs she not more cunningly ? "

Yet she held on and cut a path, and then

Our sisters followed her, till climbing grew

A common thing, and one brave life aimed high

Had lifted higher many another life.

While in her children's childhood ever young,

Fair Myra bent again and yet again

Over the cradle filled with such rich freight,

Time writ no envious wrinkles on her brow.

That gracious, gentle woman was a tomb

For scandal, and a sounding rock for praise.

Thora stood sponsor to her eldest child,

The eager Una, sending her at length

To the College she had share in shaping forth

And ruling, latest fruit of the new age ;

Glad that the longings she had longed in vain

Were satisfied for happier girls than she.

But Una never guessed her mother lived

Six months ere Thora saw the light, so worn

And faded looked the old maid by the wife.

The autumn of her life drew on, that hushed

The joyous carol of the summer birds,

Soaring on light wing into clearest heaven.

And born of August's thirsty heat came forth,

With restless buzz, myriads of stinging gnats,

Unnumbered stings of vain regret and buzz

Of countless petty cares in middle life.

Youth's dreams die hard, but find a grave at last

In silence, as the noiseless years move swift,

Each swifter than the last, till all is still.

Dusty routine dulls mind and heart, and life

Grows tame, as the great river's final reach

Far from the foam and fury of its rise

Among the hills that look towards the sun.

She has outlived girlhood's desire to know

And keen enthusiasm for high thought ;

She has outlived the hungering to do

Deeds that should echo down the aisles of Time ;

And even the craving for the cup of love

Dashed from her lips ere sipped, the dumb heart-
    ache

Missing man's love to lean on and child's love

To lean on her, a woman's deepest need.

She has not what she might havé had ; worse
    loss,

She is not what she might have been. They say,

Marking ungainly harshness in old maids,

Like o'er-ripe fruit that shrivels up unplucked,

" None would desire such women." Rather say,

" Theirs was the unlit sky of solitude.

Such women wedded prove as perfect souls

As others mellowed by warm suns of home."

And faded was the vision of God's love

Shining upon her on that holy eve.

Life's best was not her lot, but hers was much

Which other women, missing what she missed,

Possessed not : well-filled purse and wide repute,

High place, congenial work, and friendly friends.

So sought she sisters poorer than herself;

Ellen, for instance, with her scanty means

And toilsome life despite her gentle birth.

Thora and she breathed first in one bright June ;

But she, the village parson's eldest child,

Made honest effort in a little groove,

Shut out from much that girls deserving less

Took as bare right—of culture, luxury,

Leisure, and adulation—nor complained ;

Patient bread-winning filling all her days,

In Myra's cheerful schoolroom mainly spent.

Until her slender stock of lore and health

Ran dry, and all her kinsfolk passed away,

And Myra sent their youngest child to school,

Finding for her a pension and one room.

Now thither came, as to a sanctuary,

Souls held in debt or bondage or distress ;

Comfortless trouble of the needy won

Hearing and soothing ; and a benison

Flowed forth on many whom she humbly deemed

Were blessing her by visiting her couch.

Of such was Thora, pointed to by men

As one who made the new age what it is

Whose "Woman's Call" had proved a powerful hand

To lift the car of progress from the ruts

Of time-worn custom, till the Toy and Drudge

Of centuries become the crownèd Queen.

Thora was one of many a moving force

Acting on many ; Ellen for a few

Was the impelling power of their lives.

And Thora loved her well, and told to her

At length, one day, the story of her life.

Then she who never chose the words that sound

Sweet to the hearer, murmured with a tear

And kiss, " 'Twas truly, nobly, rarely done.'

And Thora lived upon that comfort long.

" Honours list headed by a woman : " text

For a discourse from Thora's facile pen

Till daylight languished with her thoughts thereon.

Then she stepped forth, the lines upon her brow

Writ deep with trace of quest unsatisfied,

For heartening converse with the gentle friend

Whose pallid face said, "Peace and joy have come

As inmates, not as passing guests to me."

Ellen in deepening dusk she found alone.

"'Tis double joy to see you on a day

I have not crossed the threshold." "Well I know'

Dear friend, whose ailing grieves me to the soul,

That, be it here or with the church's choir,

When twilight comes, you sing your evensong."

"Ay, song indeed, for when I go to God

Praise must prevent petition, as I name

The loving-kindness He hath given me

According to His mercies, finding still

Far more to thank Him than to ask Him for."

(They sat in darkness, talking with hearts bare,

As chiefest friends bare not their hearts in light.,

"Ellen, you shame my praise perfunctory.

We both have missed the woman's highest joy;

Otherwise, life has had few pangs for me,

And many pangs for you. Yet from your lips

A daily pæan of thanksgiving swells,

While I can seldom reach a mere content."

" Is there indeed a worse and better lot,

When all our lots are shaped by Love Supreme ? "

" The All-wise Potter maketh not to mar,

But surely we may thwart God's purposes,

Failing to see or heedless of His Will."

" Nay, Thora, you are loyal to our God."

" God's service has been in my lips and thoughts,

But all I tried to do had still been done

To happier issues through a nobler aim

Had I ne'er been. The girlhood of to-day

Grows on the new-cleared soil, but my rash hand,

Plucking up weeds, has haply torn away

Some modest but most fragrant flowers too :

Gentleness, tenderness, meek piety.

They called me learned Thora, but methinks

The meanest woman who has loved and known

Husband's companionship and borne a child

Hath wider outlook upon real life,

Learning in schools whose doors are closed to me.

I, doing good work ill, have hindered those

Who else had done it well. I fondly dreamed

God hired me for the service of His world,

But He may yet disown my faulty task."

" I too have plied for hire through weary hours,

Until in bondage I found liberty.

The hireling's task and meed were all too mean

For God to give His servants." Thora said,

" Unriddle this dark saying, O my friend."

" I can but say the lesson God has taught

Line upon line in simplest words to me,"

Said Ellen. " Know the hireling owns himself,

Selling his labour at his will for wage.

The bondman cannot sell himself or his ;

Being purchased by another, all his life

Is ordered for him, all his service due

When, where, and howsoe'er his owner wills.

O depth of misery when man to man

Is bondman ! But what height of bliss when we,

Bought by the blood of the Unspotted Lamb,

Yield ourselves wholly unto God's good Will,

To use as God can use the wholly given ;

Leaving us free to give or to withhold,

Since sovereign will is that which makes us men !

Now to His greater glory and our joy,

He works His loving purposes for man

Through man alone, using the yielded soul.

Were all His servants given thus to Him,

Soon all on earth would do our Master's will."

Said Thora, " Means to accomplish, seen results,

Are not true measure of our work for God.

While I have burnished candlesticks and shaped

More cunning lamps within God's holy House,

You have made human hearts true ' Ariels,'

True 'hearths of God,' * by kindling altar flames

From fires aglow within you evermore."

" God's ways are not our ways.   When first I gave

Me wholly unto God, and power asked

To serve Him more than ever heretofore,

* Isaiah xxix. 1, R.V.

He laid His hand upon me and removed

My only riches, health to earn my bread.

So I was like the king who cried of old,

' Lord, I would fight for Thee.   But how go forth

Shorn of the mighty army I had hired

With all those toil-won talents for Thy war ? '

And still the man of God said, ' Go.   Be strong,

With God to friend, for He can give much more

Than all that host to thee.'   So has He given

New wealth of friends, new work of comforting

Sad hearts with comfort that had heartened me.

For God is ever better than our hopes,

And saves us from the fears He puts to shame.

Give yourself wholly into His dear hands,

And He will bless you with best work for Him."

Then Thora went her way and sat alone,

While epoch-making thoughts whirled through her brain ;

Till midnight hush had fallen upon the town.

The archer sleeps not with his bowstring taut.

So Thora, ere she laid her down to rest,

Seeking for aught to bear her thoughts away

From self and daily work and London's air,

Opened a book at random on this tale,

From o'er the Atlantic fifty years ago.

" Two thousand souls throng in the market place,

Keen buyers and a curious crowd at gaze ;

And in the midst a maid exceeding fair,

In the first radiant dawn of womanhood.

Great eyes whose passionate appeal shines out

Through lashes on a rich-hued velvet cheek ;

A tall, lithe form instinct with health and grace.

Marble one moment, fear has stiffened limbs

And snatched away her breath ; the next, a tide

Of crimson shame mantles her queenly neck.

For know one sixty-fourth of all her blood

Is African, and for that helpless sin

Food of those hungry pitiless eyes she stands,

Sold like a filly or a heifer, mould

Of flesh and blood for pleasure or for gain

To whoso pays her price to the harsh hag,

Jealous of her handmaiden's winsomeness.

That price goes up till none can bid again

Save two—a short-necked man with forty years

Of slavery to sin writ on his face,

Who eyes her like a beast of prey, with skill

' Of serving Satan which the beasts have not ;

And a young man whose still pale face conceals

His thoughts upon that peerless damsel's doom,

Unavenged outrage, unrequited toil.

She cannot suffer wrong, since cruel taint

In her proud English blood leaves her no rights.

He hears the coarse appraisement of her charms,

Flinching.   These traffickers in human woe

Call themselves Saxons, Freedom's only heirs !

Call themselves Christ's, released from swaddling
       bands

Of superstition into broadest day !

Half his whole wealth is staked upon his bid ;

The dealer bids again, an evil smile

Of triumph on his lips ; the trembling girl

Grasps air for aught to let the life-tide out

From her white side before he calls her his,

And agonising like a drowning wretch,

Turns her dark eyes upon the younger man.

Once more he bids, the dealer leers and flees ;

And as her buyer o'er her swooning bends,

The seller says, " Well, you have got her cheap.

What will you do with your fair bargain now ? "

Then, with the light of Christ upon his face,

That true knight answers, " I shall set her free." *

Next morning Thora rose betimes and went

To meet Christ in the hush of His own day.

And kneeling at the banquet of His grace,

Sighted a summit of the hill of God

Unseen at lower levels of the ascent.

" I cried in wayward girlhood, ' God, be mine ;

God, make me happy, I will serve Thee well.'

In womanhood, I took the love of God

* See *Review of Reviews*, September 1891. The incident took
place in May 1834, and was related by the Rev. Calvin Fairbanks.

For my rich, satisfying heritage ;

And from the soils that fed them not I plucked

My fibres of affection painfully ;

Praying that they might root in the rich earth

Of God's great lovingkindness unto me.

But now, as Shulammith's first rapturous cry,

' Lo, my Beloved is mine and I am his,'

Led to a deeper joy and higher life,

' Lo, I am my Beloved's and his desire

Is toward me,' so I learn a better prayer.

'Give' cannot bring the blessing brought by
    'Take.'

Doubly Thy creature—born Thy child, since Thou

Art Father of our spirits ; bought again,

Since Thou art our Redeemer—I am Thine

By deed of gift I sign and seal to-day.

Take me and use me where and how Thou wilt ;

Work out Thy will through my surrendered will.'

Rapt in devotion, Thora hid her eyes,

But through the reverent quiet of the church

The bitter cry of bartered flesh and blood

Rang in her ears ; the vision of the mart

Haunted her eyes, with all once heard or read

Of wrongs to helpless, dusky sons of Ham,

Shipped into toilsome exile by the greed

Of men more savage and more strong than
    they,

Their bodies given to whip and manacle,

Their souls to dumb revenge and baffled hate

And lawless impulse, raging uncontrolled

In men degraded by unlawful bonds.

" 'Tis one of earth's huge sorrows, buried now.

Ere I was born their cry went up to God,

Who hates oppression, and defends the poor.

Loudly He spake to Britain, and she rose

And cut that cancer from her commonwealth.

Later, a sister-nation purged the blot

By awful war of kin 'gainst kin, in strife

Righteous as when the sons of Levi ran

Through Israel broken loose and likening God

To ox that eateth grass, with blades whence
  dripped
Their brethren's blood for sacrificial gore.
But is not Britain to dark Africa,
Which she made darker, deep in debt henceforth?
And what is darkness, for mankind or man,
Save God unknown, sin seated on the throne,
Here fair and cultured, foul and savage there,
With misery and death for its viziers?
Light and salvation, for mankind or man,
Is God known, and His will that all were saved
From sin, known also. Sin, with its desire
Towards man's ruin, coucheth at the door,
But Christian man or state rules over it,*
For Christ and righteousness are on the throne.
What part of Britain's debt is paid by me?"
So Thora asked " Who goes to Africa
To disannul her covenant with death?"
And stilled her heart's importunate appeal

* Gen. iv. 7, R.V.

Filling their hands with gold for their crusade.

Then, waking as from dream to daily work,

" Uses of higher culture claims my pen.

They say the world is over full to-day

Of learned women.   Where can all find scope

Whom culture goads to storm the towers of
    thought ? "

She halted, as she sought for a reply.

Then came the summons, " Hear what God has
    wrought

Through heralds whom your gold sent on their
    way."

She followed secretly her secret gift,

Not daring to believe that those who tread

In footsteps of the honoured Twelve to-day

Are more than untaught, misled fanatics.

The world knows not its heroes, and the Church

Blinded by dust of strife has failed to see

How Christlike 'tis to seek the furthest lost.

But how they shamed her poor, unworthy thoughts,

Those heroes, telling the unvarnished tale

They knew not for heroic, of men's hearts

Hungering for God and satisfied in Christ,

And witnessing anew for His great Name,

   y lives transformed and households born again.

She heard of perils faced in dauntless quest

Of souls, and cried, " Oh, would I were a man,

To do and dare and suffer thus for God ! "

She heard of true yokefellows to these men,

Women who laboured in the gospel too.

And cried, " Would I were young and could go
      forth !

Life were worth living unto such an end."

She heard appeal, " Come, give ye to the work

Not yours, but you.   We need more men to
      preach ;

Yet more we need the women to instruct

Women and children as they only can.

We need the vigorous youth for enterprise,

The ripe experience that may ease our toil

By care and counsel, Here is work for all."

Thora bowed head, " I am Thine handmaid, Lord

Tell me if I can serve Thee better there

Than here, and I will go forthwith for Thee."

Then in her heart a still small voice spake thus :

" Daughter, to whom no ties of home were given

Thou meekly tookest here the second place.

But thine shall be the bliss of following now,

Unhindered by such ties, the conquering Lamb

Whithersoe'er He goeth, and to thee

God will restore the years the locusts ate

Of vain ambition and of vain regret.

Thus working for His world, that needs the aid

Of all His true ones, life's best happiness

Unselfish labour to a glorious end

Is thine, and thine the everlasting name

Of builder of the human House of God."

Part VII

REST

EVENING is sweet when all the western sky
Flushes in farewell to the sun, and winds
Sweep lightly o'er the treetops ; all is still
Save drowsy cattle lowing homeward bound,
And twittering birds choosing out twigs whereon
To ruffle up their bosoms for repose.
And eventide is sweetest when the day
Knew cloud and fog, rough rain and cutting blast.
So sweet was Thora's eventide, which ends
This tale of one of many unwed lives
Lived in our midst, lighted by no romance,
No glow of passion, blazing suddenly
To ecstasy, then flickering to despair.

When the world knew how she had journeyed
    forth
They doubted, then they wagered she'd return
In six months, armed with matter for a book
To take the town by storm : but on she stayed.
And then two ancient gossips shook their heads,
" Know you not how her mother's mother died ?
'Tis maddest freak of a mad family."
What the world said had never weighed with her,
And now 'twas less than nothing.   On her way
She went ; the world went likewise on its way,
Forgetting soon that she had ever been,
For hers was service bringing no renown.
'Twas she whose healing skill brought back from
    death
Two pioneers who spent themselves too soon
In their young faith and all-adventurous zeal ;
And they were makers of a Christian state
Hereafter, which amazed the curious world.
Twas she who eased the cares of motherhood

For the brave helpmeets of those pioneers.

Twas she whose pen, none of its cunning lost

Now it was wholly God's, wrote home the tale

That stirred the hearts of Christian men to give

Themselves and theirs to battle in the van ;

That stopped the mouths of godless cavillers,

Whose ill reports of Christ's great work abroad

Battened on ignorance and apathy.

Now, her hair whitened, and her strength dried

    up

By tropic suns, she only mourns that youth

Knew not the joy of offering to this cause,

And winning store of love unknown before

As friend and counsellor of all that band.

Nor went she songless. Love must ever sing.

Full chorus in the new-clad woods of June

Yields when they don their deepest green, a while

Before they blaze upon their funeral pyre,

To the bright warble of the robin, heard

When lordlier songs are hushed in harvest time.

Such was the song of Thora's life, for such

The love of childless woman for a child.

Two precious children shared her heart of hearts,

Both at the font were held by her to seek

Admission to Christ's flock ; her daily prayer,

As fervent as a mother's, rose for them.

One was a lovely blue-eyed English girl,

With hair like fairest silk from new cocoons,

Lapped up in luxury since first she breathed,

For she was Gerald's firstborn.　Twenty years

And more he waited for his heart's first love ;

But then his kinsfolk said, " You, brotherless,

Go heirless.　Shall your ancient name die out ? "

So Gerald asked for Una, newly come

From college.　Yes, her world has learned to say,

" Let women study what they will, unblamed."

Unlike the world upon whose closèd doors

Of culture Thora once had knocked in vain.

Then pretty Una's heart and head made Home

A gracious word for Gerald day by day.

"Let Cousin Thora name our child," she said,

"And call her home for the babe's baptism."

So Thora took the hand she had not clasped

For five-and-twenty years, and knew herself

As white-haired woman happier than the girl

Who dreamed of love that far-off summer morn.

"Know Africa is heir to all my gold,

But little Thora's be the rest of mine,

And God's best blessing dwell on her and hers."

She pled for Africa in words that reached

Hearts never reached before, and turned to go.

And when she gained her equatorial home,

They claimed her mercy for another babe,

Telling this tale to her compassionate heart :—

A fettered gang pursued their painful way,

Most wretched journey to more wretched goal.

A week before, hunters of human prey

Had burst upon their village and had slain

Stalwart and sick and aged, leading off

The helpless crowd of women, lads, and babes,

In one long line of sad captivity,

Towards the coast, where all were sold as slaves

That had not died by reason of the way.

One woman, newly widowed, bore her babe,

And to her clung another child bereft,

Whose mother bled on his dead father's breast

In yonder smoking homestead.   As her steps

Faltered, the Arab driver of the gang

Muttered, " Her strength suffices not for two.

The child sells better than the babe."   So snatched

Her nursling from her, hurling it afar

Like refuse to the tangled jungle's heart.

Frantic, the fettered mother sprang on him,

And vexed at her polluting heathen touch,

He smote her to the death—one more sad soul

Dying in utter darkness in God's world,

Because His servants let the devil reign.*

* The Rev. Herbert Clarke (Universities Mission) tells this story. The Arab, however, slew the child with a stone instead of throwing it into the jungle.

Our heavenly Father heard the outcast's wail,

And guided succouring Christians to the spot.

So in the same kind arms that lately held

The dainty Lady Thora, that black babe

Took refuge.   Him she called Nathanael—

That is, in Hebrew tongue, "the gift of God."

When he laid palm to palm in childish prayer

Beside her knee, giving her more and more

The strong impulsive love of his hot race,

She wept, but not the bitter tears once shed

O'er golden-headed Eric.   Tears of joy,

Praying he might prove guileless and be blest

To all his tribe ; and thus it came to pass.

Her mind, enriched with many-coloured spoil,

Trained his mind, not less able than her own,

Until he proved to a gainsaying world

That God respects not persons when He gives

Powers that sway the hearts of other men.

He learned and taught and laboured in the Lord,

Till as "a godly and well-learned man,"

He in the stately Minster bowed his head
And rose chief shepherd of his distant flock ;
To build on soil where the white man had laid
Foundations, as the white man cannot build ;
That savage Africa be won to Christ
And sweet civility by words which won
Britain, as dark ten centuries ago.

    But Thora only saw that day by faith ;
For when her work was done God called her home.
The night wind moans amid the kingly palms,
Stirring their shadowy crowns, and earth revives
Faint from the blazing day and stifling blast
Across the desert sands.   The damp mists rise
From steaming, sodden undergrowth that chokes
The boundless, pathless forest ; all its trees
Strangled in the embrace of wandering vines
And thorny creepers, binding bough to bough,
And flinging meshes of tough greenery
Athwart the single wriggling track that led
To the lone mission-house where Thora lay.

Her comrades slept the broken sleep that comes

To arduous toilers even in this hot land ;

The howl of the hyena questing prey,

The fitful gnawing of the audacious rat,

The whirr and thud of distant gongs that made

Night hideous, keeping hideous things at bay,

Tortured her ears as she tossed to and fro,

Too spent with thirst and weakness even to pray,

Nearing the last hour of her earthly life,　　　　　　*

All her soul going out in one desire :—

" Oh, for a glimpse of dewy turf alert

With laughing daisies, for a single waft

From hawthorn hedge or thymy slope, before

I close my eyes and ears for aye, where all

Is strange, save the white moonbeam and the sob

Of the dear sea, whose distant soothing plash

I hear as its long roll comes slowly in !

The one vast sea, that washes with bright waves,

Brimful of life, the shores of all the world ;

Great highway of the nations, that at last

Brings face to face all those whom God hath made

Brothers, to serve each other ; deep and wide

As is the Love of Him at whose behest

Its tides move ceaseless, singing happy songs

To peaceful night beneath the moon's calm sway."

Her thought flies back to radiant dreams of youth

By moonlit seas, when life's untrodden path

Seemed endless, which had proved so strait and
    brief.

A headstrong girl, she lifted heart to God,

As eaglets to the great sun lift their eyes,

Yet in the nest, and knowing they must go

Sunward, but never having spread their wings ;

And cried, " Give knowledge, and I ask not love ;

Let its red roses bloom on other brows.

Give me to know Thy wisdom and Thy works."

The proud petition of a hungry mind.

In womanhood, her heart had gauged its need,

Knowledge could never fill it ; yet in strength

God-given, she renounced what she had prized

Beyond all else.   Lifted above herself

By sense of sacrifice, she lived to raise

Her sisters, shaping forth ideals new

For the unwed whose lives were nobly lived.

Then came the bitter, unexpected hour

Of impotent regret and vain desire ;

And now she cast herself on God indeed,

As eagle casts himself on yielding air,

Such trust the only path to his bright goal,

And knelt beneath the Cross to seek His love

Who died to win us grace and benison ;

So His gifts satisfied her heart a while.

Again it hungered on its self-sought way,

Until she learned to ask no other gift

Than grace to give to Him who giveth all,

And went forth for the gospel's sake, and His,

To taste pure joy in seeking His lost sheep.

   And now in His good time she dies.   Strength
      fails

And thought drifts feebly on.   " Methinks I stand

At last beside a misty sea alone.

The low-hung clouds hide from my stedfast gaze

All save the waves that break upon the shore,

Murmuring : not a sound save seabird's scream.

I go alone whither my fathers went.

Behind me lie the sunny meads and cots

Where once we nested, and the rugged hills

My   daring   youth   strove   up,   the   shadowy
    streams

Where I lay weary ; all the sights and sounds

That made my life for ever far away.

And as I face the unknown sea, a voice

Whispers, ' 'Tis shoreless.'   As that lonely sail

Slips from my gaze in rolling fog, I pass

Out into nothingness : the fair, fond dream

Of life beyond this life will melt away

With tinkling church bells gathering living men

To dream it still.   O last perplexing doubt !

I fought thee once in mail of evidence,

Creed tested, book inspired, and witness given,

Armour too heavy for my weary frame
To carry now. I know not what is true.
But I know Him, the Truth, who led me on,
Through all the tangled, devious path of life.
And in His holy keeping my faint soul
Is safe, till darkness break in perfect Light."

THE END.